DRAFT YOUR OWN BUSINESS LETTERS

DRAFT YOUR OWN BUSINESS LETTERS

Kay White

GOODWILL PUBLISHING HOUSE
New Delhi - 110 008 (INDIA).

Published by
Rajneesh Chowdhry
GOODWILL PUBLISHING HOUSE
B-9, Rattan Jyoti, 18 Rajendra Place,
New Delhi - 110 008 (INDIA).
Tel - 5750801, 5755519.
Fax : 5763428.

ISBN : 81:7245:031:1

Printed at Kumar Offset Printers Ph. : 2213315

CONTENTS

CHAPTER 10
CIRCULARS

CHAPTER 11
APPLICATIONS AND APPOINTMENTS

CHAPTER 12
AGENCY DISTRIBUTORSHIP

CHAPTER 13
ENQUIRIES, QUOTATIONS AND THEIR REPLIES

CHAPTER 14
ORDERS AND THEIR EXECUTION

CHAPTER 15
CANCELLATION AND COMPLAINTS REGARDING ORDERS

CHAPTER 16
CLEARING AND FORWARDING LETTERS

CHAPTER 17
CORRESPONDENCE WITH THE RAILWAYS AND ROAD TRANSPORT COMPANIES

CHAPTER 18
CORRESPONDENCE WITH A POST OFFICE

CHAPTER 19
PAYMENTS—COLLECTIONS

CHAPTER 20
BANKING CORRESPONDENCE

CHAPTER 21
INSURANCE CORRESPONDENCE

CHAPTER 22
CORRESPONDENCE REGARDING MOTOR VEHICLES

CHAPTER 23
IMPORT & EXPORT CORRESPONDENCE

1
Essentials of a Good Business Letter

The success of any modern business, to a large extent, depends on the use of business letters. Someone has rightly said: *"A letter in business is what medicine is to a patient"*. Good letters are little ambassadors that traverse every nook and corner of the present day Commercial World. They constitute the biggest source of active liaison that is necessary concomitant for procuring business.

In the words of Mr. Herbert N. Casson: A good letter is a master key that opens locked doors. It opens markets. It opens the way for your goods or your services. It tells the story of the real character of your firm.

What does a good business letter do?

1. It sells goods.
2. It creates new customers.
3. It brings back the lost customers.
4. It brings good travelling sales-representatives.
5. It gives an incentive to the dealers.
6. It instills confidence among the suppliers.
7. It brings back confidence amongst the buyers.
8. It collects bad debts.
9. It settles disputes.
10. It brings more finance.
11. It opens new markets.
12. It brings more profits.
13. It builds the business and the nation.

LAYOUT OF A BUSINESS LETTER

Stationery. Always use the best quality paper. It should be plain and not ruled. The two most acceptable qualities of paper and Bond and Airmail. The normal size of a letterhead is 11 inches by 8½ inches and 8½ inches by 5 inches.

Colour of stationery. White paper is the best. However, some business concerns prefer to use light shades of grey, brown and blue. It may, however, be noted that bright colours like yellow, orange, green, red, etc. are never desirable.

In some large concerns different colours of stationery are used for different departments. This, of course, is a good idea as it helps to discriminate correspondence of different departments. Also, the different copies like the first copy or the second copy, etc., are sometimes made in different colours.

Typing. There is no second opinion that all business letters must be type-written. Use of two coloured ribbons (red and black or blue) for accounts, statements or similar work is recommended. Proper spacing in a further necessity and it must be carefully looked after.

Envelopes. Needless to say that an envelope is the most important part of business stationery, as your client will firstly glance at it. The quality of the envelope should correspond to the quality of the letter-head.

2

Parts of the Business Letter

A business letter is generally divided into the following six parts:—

1. The Heading
2. The Inside Address
3. The Salutation
4. The Body of Letter
5. The Complimentary Close
6. The Signature

1. Heading. It indicates when and where the letter was written and thus it comprises the postal address of the writer and the date on which the letter was written. The address may appear either in the centre or on the right-hand side of the letter. The date, however, generally appears on the right-hand side. Proper spacing between the name of the firm and its address and between the address and the date is of paramount importance. A few examples of a heading are give below:

A. **JOHNSON TRADING COMPANY**
18-Prince of Wales Street,
London 3132 1A.
(U.K.)

Date............19................

B. **JOHNSON TRADING COMPANY**
18-Prince of Wales Street,
London 3132 1A.
(U.K.)

Date............19................

C. **JOHNSON TRADING COMPANY**
18-Prince of Wales Street,
London 3132 1A.
(U.K.)

Date............19................

Note: It is necessary to write "London (U.K.)", when the letter is communicated between U.K. and another country.

2. Inside Address. This comprises name and address of a person of the firm to whom the letter is written and appears on the left-hand side of the letter. This corresponds to the address on the envelope with the only difference that in some cases, the number and name of the street is omitted. This, however, is unwise and a complete address is always desirable, as otherwise, it may become difficult to locate a reference with the copy of the letter. Proper spacing and punctuation are necessary here as well.

The word *Messrs* is generally prefixed to a partnership firm or "& Co."

EXAMPLE

Messrs. Kepler Bros.,
Boston (USA)

The above address on the letter is not sufficient. The better way to write the address is:

Messrs. Kepler Bros.,
12, West Side Street,
Boston 313 (USA)

3. Salutation. This appears below the name and the address of the recipient (to whom the letter is written).

The various words used as salutations are:— *Sir, Dear Sir, Sirs, Madam, Gentlemen, Dear Mr.* ——, *Dear Miss* —— , *Dear Mrs.* —— .

A salutation in business is followed by a *comma* (,)

Sir,: This has become very formal now-a-days and is not generally used except by Government offices.

Dear Sir,: This is by far the most accepted form of salutation. However, this is used only when the relationship between the correspondents already exists.

Dear Sirs,: This type of salutation is used in case of letters addressed to companies or partnership firms where the word *Messrs* is generally used, and where the letter is addressed to a Firm and not to the Manager or any other person.

Dear Miss, Dear Mrs., Dear Mr.: These are used only where the writer knows the recipient well and wants to give a personal (friendly) touch rather than being formal as usual.

4. Body of the Letter. It is that portion of the letter which contains the message or the information which the writer wants to communicate.

The body of the letter should be divided into different paragraphs. Each subject should be dealt within a separate paragraph.

The first paragraph should introduce the subject-matter of the letter and where it is a reply, the reference number and date should be clearly mentioned. In the subsequent paragraphs, different topics may be discussed.

5. The Complimentary Close. This should always agree with salutation and it must always be followed by a *comma.* The most common forms of complimentary close are:

1. Yours faithfully,
2. Yours truly,
3. Yours very truly,
4. Yours respectfully,
5. Yours sincerely,
6. Yours obediently,
7. Your obedient servant, (This form is now seldom used.)

Examples of suitable complimentary close to saluations are:—

Dear Sir,	Yours faithfully, or Yours truly,
Dear Madam,	Yours faithfully, or Yours truly,
Dear Sirs,	Yours faithfully, or Yours truly,
Sir	Your obedient servant,
Madam,	Your obedient servant,
Gentlemen,	Yours obedient servant,
My dear Sir,	Yours very truly,
My dear Sirs,	Yours very truly,

Dear Madam,	Yours very truly,
Dear Mr.,	Yours sincerely,
Dear Miss,	Yours sincerely,
Dear Mrs.,	Yours sincerely,

6. Signature. The complimentary close will be followed by the signature of the writer. As far as possible, the signature should be legible, otherwise the name of the writer should be typed. In some cases, the name of the firm or the company is also mentioned immediately after the complimentary close, but before the signature. Designation of the writer may also be used wherever possible.

3
Commercial Abbreviations

A

A-1	first class
@	at the rate of
a.a.r.	against all risks
abbr.	abbreviation
abbrev.	abbreviation
abr.	abridged
abs.	absent
abstr.	abstract
a/c	account
A/C	Account
ac.	account
acct.	account
A.D.	Acknowledgement Due
a.d.	after date
	anno domini: in the year of our Lord
Ad lib.	*Ad libitum* (At pleasure)
ad lib.	*ad libitum* (at pleasure)
admin.	administration
ad. val.	*ad valorem* (according to value)
ad.	advertisement
advt.	advertisement
Advt.	Advertisement
advert.	advertisement
aftn.	afternoon
agcy.	agency
agt.	agent
Agt. Agent	
alt.	alternate

alt.	altitude
alt.	altogether
A.M.	*Ante Meridiem* (Morning) (Before Noon)
a.m.	*ante meridiem* (morning) (Before noon)
amt.	amount
a/o	account of
appro.	approval
Arith	Arithmetic
art.	article
A/S	account sales or sales account
assn.	association
assoc.	association
asst.	assistant
asst.	assorted
Aug.	August
aux.	auxiliary
Ave.	Avenue

B

bal.	balance
b.b.	bill book or bank book
bd.	board
bd.	bound
B.C.	Before Christ
B/E	Bill of Exchange
bdl.	bundle
bdth.	breadth
b.f.	brought forward
bk.	bank
bk.	book
b.k.	book-keeping
B/L	bill of Lading
b/I	bill of lading
bl.	barrel
bl.	bale

bldg.	building
blk.	bulk
blk.	blank
bot.	bottle
B.P.	Bill Payable
bp.	bill of parcel
b.p.	boiling point
b.p.	below proof
B.R.	Bills Receivable
B/R.	Bills Receivable
Br.	Brother, Branch
brl.	barrel
bro.	brother
B.S.	Bill of Sale
B/S	Bill of Sale
b.s.	balance sheet
bt.	bought
bght.	bought
bu.	bushel (s)
bu.	bureau
bx.	box

C

C.	Centigrade/cents
C.A.	Chartered Accountant/ Cost Accountant
ca.	*circa* (about)
cap.	capital
cap.	capitalize
capt.	captain
c.c.	carbon copy
cc.	cubic centimetre(s)
C.E.	Civil Engineer
cent.	centigrade
cent.	centimetre
cent.	a hundredth
cf.	refer

cge. p.d	carriage paid
C.H.	Custom House
chem.	chemical
chg.	charge
chgd.	charged
chm.	chemical
chron.	chronological
Cie.	Compaigne
c.i.f.	cost, insurance and freight
C/L.Carload	
c.l.	cart-load
cml.	commercial
Co.	Company
co.	company
c.o.	care of
C/o	care of
C.O.D.	Cash on Delivery
c.o.d.	cash on delivery
Col.	Colonel, column
comp.	compound
comm.	commission, communication
consgt.	consignment
cont.	continued
contr.	contract
Co-op.	Co-operative (Society)
Corpn.	Corporation
corr.	correspondence
c.p.	candle power
Cp.	Compare
cpd.	compound
Cr.	Creditor
cr.	creditor
cr.	credit
C/R.	Company's Risk
c/s.	cases
ct.	carat

cu.	cubic
cum. div.	with dividend
currt.	current
current	present month or year
C.W.O.	Cases with order
Cwt.	hundred weight

D

D	In Roman numerals, 500
d.	date
d/a.	document against acceptance
d/d.	days after date
d/d	delivered
Dec.	December
deg.	degree(s)
del.	deliver
del.	delegate
dely.	delivery
dept.	department
deptt.	department
dis.	discount
disc.	discount
disct.	discount
Ditto	The same
div.	dividend
div.	division
divd.	dividend
dk.	dock
dk.	dark
dks.	docks
D/-	Debit note
do.	ditto (the same)
D/o	delivery order
doz.	dozen
d/p.	documents against payment
dpth.	depth
Dr	Debtor

dr.	debtor/debit
dr.	dram
dr.	drawer
d.s.	days after sight
d/s.	days after sight
dup.duplicate	
dy.	delivery
dz.	dozen

E

ea.	each
ed.	edited
ed.	edition
ed.	editor
EE.	Errors Excepted
e.g.	*exempli gratia* (for example).
encl.	cenclosure
encls.	enclosures
E. & O.E.	errors and omissions excepted
e.o.m.	end of month
eq.	equal
equit	equivalent
Esq.	Esquire
est.	establish
est.	estimate
et.al.	*et alibate* (and elsewhere)
etc.	etcetera (and so forth and the rest)
et Cie	& Compaigne
et. seq.	*et sequent* (and the following)
ex.	from
ex.	example
ex.	exchange
exc.	exchange
exec.	exclusive
exec.	executive
ext.	extension
ex. div.	ex dividend (without dividend)

F

F.	Friday/Fahrenheit
f.a.a.	free of all average
fac.	facsimile
facs.	facsimile
fah.	fahrenheit
f.a.q.	fair average quality
f.a.s.	free alongside ship
f.d.	free docks (goods to be delivered)
Feb.	February
fig.	figure
f.o	folio
f.o.b.	free on board
F.O.B.	Free on Board
fol.	folio
folg.	following
F.O.R.	Free On Rail
f.p.	foot-pound
f.p.a.	free particulars average (marine insurance)
fr.	franc
Free case	no charge for case
Fri.	Friday

G

gal.	gallon
gall. gallon	
g.c.f.	greatest common factor
gds.	goods
gen.	general
gm.	gramme
gns.	guneas
Gr.	Grains
Gr.	Gross
gr. wt.	gross weight
gro. wt.	gross weight

grs.	gross.
g.t.c.	good till cancelled
guar.	guaranteed
g.v.	*grandle votesse* (Fast goods train)

H

hhd.hogshead	
Hon.	Honourable
hon.	honorary
H.P.	Horse Power
h.p.	horse power
H.P.	Hire Purchase
h.p.n.	horse power nominal
hr.	hour
hrs.	hours
ht.	heat
ht.	height

I

ib.	*ibidem* (in the same place)
ibid.	*ibidem* (in the same place)
i.c.	in charge
i.d.	*idem* (the same)
i.e.	*idest* (that is)
I.H.P.	indicated horse power
imp.	important
imp.	imported
in.	inch
inc.	incorporated
Inc.	Incorporated
inc.	including
inc.	incomplete
incorp.	Incorporated
in ex.	in extenso
inf.	information
inf.	*infra* (below)

ins.	insurance
inst.	instant (present month)
int.	interest
inv.	invoice
I/O.	inspecting order
I.O.U.	I owe you
ital	*italics*

J

Jan.	January
jn.	Junction
J.P.	Justice of the Peace
Jr.	Junior
Jun	June
Jul.	July
Jt.	Joint
J.S.	Joint Secretary

K

k.	kilo
k.g.	kilogramme
kild.	kilderkin
k.m.	kilometre
k.o.	knock out
kt.	carat
kw.	kilowat (s)

L

L.	In Roman numerals, 50
£ or l.	A pound Sterling
lb.	A pound weight
L/C.	Letter of Credit
Lib.	Library
Lim.	Limited
Lit.	Litre
lgth.	length
log.	logarithm

Ltd.	Limited
ltd.	limited
lugg. rail	goods train

M

m.	minute
m.	month
m.	metre
maj.	major
Mar.	March
max.	maximum
m/d.	months after date
mdse.	merchandise
med.	medium
mem.	member
memo.	memorandum
Messrs.	Messieurs
mfg.	manufacturing
mfr.	manufacture
mfr.	manufacturer
m.g.	milligram
Mgr.	Manager
mgr.	manager
Mks.	marks
min.	minimum
min.	minute
misc.	miscellaneous
M.M.	Messieurs
m.m.	millimetre
M.O.	Money Order
m.o.	money order
Mon.	Monday
m.p.h.	mile per hour
Mr.	Mister
M/s.	messrs
Mrs.	Mistress
Ms.	Manuscript

MS.	manuscript
ms.	manuscript
m/s.	months after sight
mths.	months
mos.	months
mts.	minutes
Mtge.	mortgage

N

n.	north/nitrogen
n.a.	not available/not applicable
N.B.	*nota bene* (mark well)
neg.	negative/negligible
nem. con.	no one objecting
No.	number
no.	number
nom. cap.	nominal capital
Nov.	November
nr.	near
n.s.	not specified

O

O.	Order
o.	order
o.a.	on account (of)
O/a.	on account (of)
o.c.	Overcharge, office copy
o.d.	on demand
O.I.G.S.	On India Government Service
op. cit.	*opere citato* (in the work or book cited)
o.s.	out of stock
%	per cent
oz.	ounce

P

p.	per or through
p.a.	per annum
p.c.	per cent

pcl.	parcel
pd.	paid
per ann.	per annum
per pro.	per procuration; by proxy
pkg.	packing
P & L.	Profit and loss
p.m.	*post meridiem* (after noon)
P.N.	Promissory Note
P.O.	Postal Order/Poster Office
pp.	pages
P.P.	Parcel Post/Particular Person (Telephone)
pro.	for
pro. tem.	tem. for the time being
Prox.	Proximo, Next month
P.T.O.	Please turn over
P.V	*Petit Vitesse* (Ordinary goods train)

Q

q.v.	*quod vide* (which see)
qual.	quality
qy.	query

R

Re.	Refer or referring to
re.	refer or referring to
recd.	received
recpt.	receipt
regd.	registered
refce	reference
reg.	registered
retd.	returned
retd.	retired
R.P.	reply paid
R.S.V.P.	*respondez s'il vous plait* (reply, if you please)

S

S.	Shilling
S/d.	Sight draft

Sec.	Secretary
sec.	secretary, second
senr.	senior
sh.	shilling
S.N.	Shipping Note
Sq.	Square
Sq. ft.	Square foot
Sq. yd.	Square yard
Sr.	Senior
SS.	Steamship
S/S	Steamship
Stg.	Sterling
Str.	steamer
Subs. cap.	subscribed capital

T

T.L.O.	total loss only
gm.	telegram
tr.	tare (weight)

U

ult.	ultimo (last month)
U.K.	United Kingdom
U.S.A.	United Staes of America
U.S.S.R	Union of Soviet Socialist Republics

V

via.	By way of
V.P.L.	Value Payable Letter
V.P.P.	Value Payable Post
viz.	namely

W

wt.	weight
w.e.f.	with effect from

Y

yd.	yard
yr.	year

4

Avoid the Use of Certain Phrases

Instead of	*Use*
At all times	Always
As per	According to
Anticipating your reply	We shall look forward with interest to your reply
Awaiting your esteemed instructions	We shall wait for your reply
At your earliest convenience	Please reply as soon as possible
Above mentioned	Referred to above
Enclosed herewith	Enclosed
Have noted its contents	Avoid using this phrase
In accordance with your request	As requested by you
If you will refer to your file	Please refer to your file
Kindly advise	Please let us know
The said shipment	The shipment
We take this opportunity	Avoid using this phrase
We wish to thank you	We thank you
We would recommend	We recommend
We would suggest	We suggest
We beg to acknowledge your letter of	We thank you for your letter of
We acknowledge with thanks your letter of	We thank you for your letter of
We beg to state	We would like to state
We would like to be advised	Please let us know
We are this day writing	We are writing today

You have our permission	You may
Your valued instructions	Your instructions

5

Words Commonly Mis-spelt

Given below is a list of words commonly used in business correspondence but mis-spelt by many. While keeping a standard dictionary is always an advantage. The following ready-made list will go a long way in saving time in referring to dictionary every now and then.

A

absence
absurd
accelerate
accept
accidentally
accommodate
accompanying
accomplish
according
accumulate
acknowledgement
acquaintance
acquire
address
advice
advise
aggravate
allotted
allowed
all right
among
amount
analysis
annual
answer
apology
apparent
appropriate
approximate
argument
ascent
assistance
athletic
attendance
attorney
awkward

B

baggage
balance
bankruptcy
basically
becoming
beginning
believe
beneficial
book-keeper
bonded

brilliant
bureau
bushel
bulletin
business

C

campaign
canvass
casualties
certain
choose
chosen
commitment
community
comparison
complement
concede
concession
confidence
consistent
contraband
cordially
courteous
criticism
canvas
carrying
cemetery
characteristic
chose
column
committee
comparative
competitive
compliment
conceive
conference
conscientious
continuous
convenient
correlate
courtesy
crisis

D

dairy
debenture
deceitful
decision
definite
delete
desirous
desperate
develop
device
dictaphone
dilapidate
disastrous
dealt
deceive
decide
defendant
digression
description
despair
dessert
development
devise
difference
disappoint
discipline

discord
dying
discount
divide

E

efficiency
eliminate
emphasize
entirely
equivalent
essential
excellent
exccutive
existence
explanation
extraordinary
extremely
eligible
eminent
endeavour
equipment
especially
exceed
execute
exhibit
experience
extension
extravagance

F

fallacious
fascinate
February
financier
forfeit
fundamental
familiar
feasible
finally
foreign
fulfil

G

genuine
government
guess
guilt
gentleman
guarantee
guidance

H

hindrance
hyphen
hurriedly

I

identification
identity
imperative
identify
immediately
implement

inadequate
indefinitely
inevitable
instant
invariable
irrelevant
it's (contraction)
item
incidentally
indispensable
insistent
interpretation
irrecoverable
irresistible
its (possessive)

J

judicial
judgement
judicious

K

knight
knowledge

L

laboratory
lenient
licence
loose
legitimate
liable
limited
lose

M

magazine
maintenance
manufacture
material
medicine
miscellaneous
maintain
manuscript
mathematics
millionaire
modifying
mortgage

N

neither
noticeable

O

obligation
occasion
occurred
omission
opportunity
obstacle
occasionally
occurrence
omitted
original

P

pamphlet
particularly
peculiar
perceive
permanent
permissible
perseverance
persistence
personnel
persuade
possession
possibility
practically
precede
preference
prejudice
preparation
prevalent
principle
privilege
principal
probably
prominent
pronunciation
psychology
pursuit

Q

quality
quantity
question
questionnaire

R

reality
realize
recede
receipt
receive
recognize
recommended
reference
referred
relevant
repetition
representative
reservoir
resistance
respectfully
respectively

S

sacrifice
scarcely
schedule
scientific
secretary
seize
severely
significant
simultaneously
sincerely
specifically
specimen
stationery
strictly

substantial
succeed
success
summary
superintendent
supersede
surprise
suspicion
syllable
synonymous

T

tabulation
tariff
technicality
temperament
tendency
theoretically
thorough
through
transferred
treasure
truly
trustee

U

unanimous
undeveloped
undoubtedly
unnecessary
usually
utilization

V

vacancy
valuable
variety
vigilance
vigorous

W

Wednesday
wholly
who's
whose
writer
writing
written

Y

you're
yours
your

6
Words Commonly Misused

A, An — 'A' is used before a word which starts with a consonant sound while 'An' is used before a word which starts with a vowel sound e.g. — A Cashier, An Indian.

According to, In accordance with — Note of the two gives a direct expression and it is always desirable to write something natural. Thus, instead of writing 'In accordance with your request it is better to write, 'We have pleasure in sending a detailed folder you requested' etc.

Accept, Except — 'Accept' means to receive or to confirm. Except means to omit.

Acknowledge, Acknowledging — Instead of writing 'We acknowledge with thanks the receipt of your letter, or While acknowledging your letter of; it is better to use simple sentence like 'Thank you for your letter —'.

Affect, Effect — 'Affect' means to influence. 'Effect' (verb) means to cause, institute. Effect (noun) means a result.

All ready, Already — All ready means 'entirely ready' and Already means 'by this time'.

Alright, All right — It is always better to use the word 'All right' instead of 'Alright'.

All together, Altogether — 'All together' means all things or persons together while 'altogether' means 'completely'.

Among, Between — 'Among' is always used 'when the objects are three or more. 'Between' is used only when the objects are two.

Amount, Number — 'Amount' refers to 'Measurable quantity', 'Number' refers to the Countable quantity.

And, Etc. — 'And' should never be used with Etc. Thus, 'table, chair, coat, almirah, etc.' is correct.

Anticipating — Always avoid using the word 'Anticipating'. Thus 'anticipating your order' and 'anticipating your reply' are not in form.

Any place, Anywhere, Anywheres — Always use 'Any where' in place of 'any place or anywheres'.

Appraise, Evaluate, Assess — 'Appraise' and 'Evaluate' means to ascertain the value or amount of. 'Assess' means to value for tax purposes.

Approve, Endorse — 'Approve' means 'to sanction'. 'Endorse' means 'have favourable opinion'.

Apt, Likely, Liable — 'Apt' denotes natural tendency. 'Likely' means probably. 'Liable' means exposed to disadvantage or danger or legal responsibility.

As per — Use more natural expression. Thus, instead of writing 'As per your letter of' — it is better to write 'As you state in your letter,' or 'As mentioned in your letter'.

At, About — Always use about. Thus 'at about 5 p.m.' is not correct while 'about 5 p.m.' is correct.

Attached herewith — Anything attached is necessarily herewith. Say attached to this letter, not attached herewith.

Beg — It is too humble and as far as possible avoid using the same.

Beside, Besides — Beside means 'along the side of'. Besides means 'in addition to' or 'with the exception of'.

Best of Any — The expression should be best, best of those, or better than any other.

Can, May — Can means 'capability'. May means with 'permission'.

Cannot help but — Note that the 'not and the but' make a double negative. Omit but. Thus say 'cannot help'

Can't hardly — This is again a double negative. Use either 'Can't' or 'Hardly'. Thus, 'I can hardly see anything' or 'I can't see anything' have got to be written.

Cite, Sight, Site — 'Cite' means to call attention to. 'Sight' means 'something seen'. 'Site' is location.

Data — Data is a plural of datum.

Deal — Avoid using it for representing to mean 'Bargain or Transaction'.

Different than, Different from — The preferred idiom, is 'different from' and hence avoid using 'different than'.

Due to — Due is a Predicate Adjective, meaning 'due efficiency'. Do not use 'due to' in situations that can take 'because of' or 'owing to'.

Farther, Further — 'Farther' means distance. 'Further' means to an advanced degree.

Favour — Never call a letter a favour. Thus, instead of writing 'Please favour us with a reply' write 'Please send us your reply'.

Fewer Lesser — 'Fewer' used for 'Countable quantities' and 'Lesser' is used for 'Measurable quantities'.

Former, Latter — These words should be used while referring to one of the two things or persons. In all other cases, the correct usage is 'first and the last'.

Good, Well — 'Good' is generally an Adjective, while 'Well' is generally an Adverb, e.g., He is a good boy; He is getting on well with his studies.

Imply, Infer — 'Imply' means 'to express indirectly'. 'Infer' means 'to deduce'.

Irregardless, Regardless — The use of 'Irregardless' is incorrect. Always use 'Regardless'.

Kind of a, Sort of a — Avoid 'a' in both cases.

Leave, Let — 'Leave' means 'to go away from'. 'Let' means 'to allow' e.g., 'Leave me alone'; 'Let me do my job'.

Might of, Must of — Never use these words. Instead use 'Might have'; 'Must have'.

Most, All — Never use these two contradictory words. Always use 'Almost all'.

Off, of — Never use 'of' after 'off'. Thus, 'he hardly went off of the street' is incorrect. 'He hardly went off the street' is correct.

Oral, Verbal — Oral or written paper. As per verbal instructions, are correct usages.

Principal, Principle — 'Principal' means Head of an Institution or an Organisation, etc.; 'Principle' means fundamental rule.

Raise, Rise — 'Raise' means to lift up as, His salary has been raised. 'Rise' means 'to move up', Prices of many commodities have risen up.

Re — Abbreviation re. for 'regarding' should always be avoided. Use the word 'regarding instead of 're'.

Reason is because, Reason is that — The correct usage is 'reason is that', and not 'reason is because'.

Recent date — Give the exact date instead of writing 'recent date'.

Sit, Set — 'Sit' means 'to be seated'; 'set' means 'to put in position'.

Stationary, Stationery — Former means 'not moving', latter means 'writing supplies'.

This there, That there — Do not use 'there' with 'this', 'than' or those.

These kind — Since kind is singular, 'these' should not be used with it. The correct usage, therefore, is 'this kind', or 'these kinds'.

Thusly — It is an irritating word. Use 'thus' only.

We. I — The word 'we' is used when it is desired to represent a company or firm in business writing. However, when it is desired to represent or speak for an individual only, use 'I'.

7

Commercial Terms

Abandonment. The relinquishment or surrender of rights, interest or property by one person to another expressly or by implication.

Acceptance. Is the act by which the drawee of a bill of exchange binds himself to pay the same when due. Writing of the name across the face of the bill constitutes acceptance.

Account. In accounting, it means a ledger sheet showing debit and credit of any asset, liability, income, etc., while in business, every customer is sometimes referred as a separate account.

Accounts Current. Statements of accounts rendered between home firms and foreign firms, between whom there are frequent transactions, showing the daily balance and adding or deducting interest thereon.

Account Payable. A debt, owing to an enterprise, which arises in the normal course of business dealing and is not supported by negotiable paper.

Act of God. Any act beyond human causes or not subject to human foresight.

Advance Bill. A bill of exchange drawn before shipment of goods.

Ad Valorem. According to value.

Ad Valorem Duty. Duty levied on the value of certain item and can only be altered by a special resolution of the members.

At the Market. An order to a broker to sell immediately at the best possible price.

Back Bill. A statement of unpaid charges.

Bad Debt. A debt which is no more accepted to be recoverable from the debtor.

Balance Sheet. A list or statement showing the details of assets and liabilities of any organisation.

Bank Acceptance. A bill of exchange accepted by a bank for payment on the date.

Bank Note. In India, the issue of bank notes, is the monopoly of Reserve Bank of India. A bank note is a legal tender and is a promissory note payable on demand to bearer.

Bankruptcy. It is a state of insolvency in which the effects of a man unable to pay his debts are taken over by a trustee and distributed for the benefit of all his creditors.

Bill of Entry. A document describing goods before they are landed, which importers give to Customs authorities.

Bill of Exchange. It is an unconditional written order by one party ordering the latter to pay to same third party, on demand or at some future date.

Bill of Leading. A document issued by the carrier to the shipper as a receipt and as a contract governing transportation and delivery of the articles only.

Advice. A sworn statement for declaration in writing before an official authorised to execute such instruments.

After Sight. A term used to indicate that the period for which a Bill of Exchange is drawn, will not begin until after it has been presented to the drawee.

Agreement. A contract or bargain to do or not to do certain things, whereas it is always desirable to have all the agreements in writing. However, it has often been found that even verbal agreements are equally honoured by the parties concerned.

Allonge. A ship of paper pasted on a Bill of Exchange for continuation of endorsement.

All-Risk Insurance. An insurance policy insuring against loss caused by all perils except those especially excluded and are hence mentioned on the policy.

Appeal Bond. A bond required of an appellant to assure payment of costs and damages if the appeal is lost.

Article of Association. This document defines the powers, rights, duties and authority of the shareholders and the directors of a Limited Company. It is a set of rules for the internal management of the Company.

Bond. A sealed document by which a person binds himself, his heirs, executors and administrators to pay a certain sum to another person on or before a specified date.

Bonded Goods. Goods stored in a warehouse by an owner who has furnished a bond to pay duty or taxes due.

Bonded Warehouse. A government building in which bonded goods are stored.

Brand. Trade mark applied on packages, casks and other containers.

Breach of Contract. Breaking the terms of contract by non-performance or doing some such act which is contrary to the terms of the contract.

Broker. Is an agent who buys and sells on behalf of other people without taking possession of the goods.

Brokerage. It is the remuneration which is paid to the broker. It is generally a certain percentage.

Capital. It is the sum of money employed by a person or a company in a business undertaking. It is also principal of a loan.

Call Loan. Money loaned payable on call or demand. Such loans are secured by securities as these can be readily sold if the money is not paid. The limit allowed for payment before selling the securities is twenty-four hours.

Cash Discount. A discount allowed for payment of a debt in advance.

Caveat Emptor. It is a Latin phrase which means 'let the buyer beware'. In other words, all risks lie with the buyer except what constitutes fraud and certain implied warranties.

Caveat Venditor. It is a Latin phrase which means 'let the seller beware' It is used as an opposite of 'caveat emptor'.

Charter Party. A document which sets forth the agreement between parties in hiring a ship for a voyage or for a period.

Cheque. It is a bill of exchange drawn on a banker and payable on demand.

(a) Bearer Cheque. A 'bearer cheque' is one made payable to payee or bearer.

(b) Order Cheque. An 'order chaque' is one made payable to payee or order.

(c) Crossed Cheque. A 'crossed cheque' is one made payable to a payee on order.

(d) Post-dated Cheque. A 'post-dated cheque' is one in which the date inserted is a future one. In other words, it is not encashable on the date of its issue.

(e) Stale Cheque. A 'state cheque' is one that has not been presented for payment within a reasonable time. In India, any cheque not presented for payment over a period of six months from the date it bears, is a stale cheque.

Circular Note. A letter of credit issued by a bank to clients enabling the holders to obtain payment at various places abroad.

Closing Price. The price at which the last sale on an organised market is made on a particular day.

Commission. It is the remuneration paid to an agent for carrying through a transaction or introducing business.

Common Carrier. A transportation agency operating under a certificate from the government which requires the carrier to serve all the people.

Common Law. Usages and customs which have come to be sanctioned as precedents, but are not reduced to codes.

Company. It is an association of persons combined for purposes of profit, and contributing to a common capital.

Consignment. A form of bailment in which one party sends goods to another party for sale.

Contract . (Acceptance of agreement). An agreement between two or more parties for a legal purpose and supported by consideration.

Cover. Money deposited as security against possible loss.

Cover Note. A document issued by insurer giving temporary insurance cover pending the issue of a formal insurance policy.

Credit. Ability to secure goods or services in the present against the promise to pay for them in the future. In accounting, the credit side of the account is one in which receipts are entered.

Credit, letter of. A letter of credit is a letter given to a representative of an agent going abroad, instructing a banker to meet the drafts against that letter up to a specified amount.

Credit Bill. A bill of exchange where the debtor has arranged in advance for credit with the drawee.

Credit Note. It is a form which the details of reduction or rebate from an already rendered account are given.

Creditor. One to whom some debt is owed by another.

Current Account. It is an account with a bank which is maintained by a business concern for collecting and paying accounts. No interest is generally allowed on the credit balance of the current account. On the other hand if the balances of the current accounts are smaller, a charge is generally made by the bank.

Customs Duties. These are the taxes levied by the Government on certain imported and exported goods.

Date of Maturity. Date on which a debt is owed by another.

Days of Grace. Extra time allowed by law or custom for making certain payments.

Dead Stock. Inventory for which there is little or no demand.

Dead Weight. The weight of freight-carrying vehicles or vessels without load.

Debenture. A document issued under the seal of the company, usually charging all or some of a company's property in favour of the holder. The rate of interest payable the time within which the amount is to be repaid, etc. are clearly mentioned on the document.

Debit. In accounts, a debit refers to an amount for which outgoing is entered. It also means a debt or an amount owed.

Debtor. Refers to a person/firm/company which owes a certain amount.

Default. Failure to perform a term of contract at the stipulated time..

Demurrage. A charge made on the goods by railway/transport companies/shippers, etc. for retaining goods beyond a specified period.

Deposit Account. This refers to an account with the bank in which the amount is paid or deposited which is not required for an immediate use. A certain interest is paid on this sum by the bank and usually a notice for withdrawal is required.

Discount. A reduction of a principal amount.

(i) *Cash Discount* is allowed for making cash or prompt payments.

(ii) *Trade Discount* is allowed by the manufacturers or producers to their dealers. This is generally a certain percentage on the marked or printed price of the product.

(iii) *Special Discount* is allowed under special circumstances— generally on the large orders or on orders received during a particular period. In certain cases it is also allowed on shop-soiled stock.

Dishonour. Failure or refusal to make payment on note or bill of exchange when due.

Dividend. This refers to the interest paid on investment. Profits of a company divisible among its members are also dividends.

Due Bill. A written admission of a debt.

Endorsement. The writing of the holder's name on the back of a cheque or a bill of exchange in favour of another.

Excise Duty. Taxes levied by the Government on certain articles manufactured for home consumption.

Executor. A person appointed by a will to see that its provisions are duly carried out.

Express Warranty. A statement of conduct by a seller to a buyer that a specific condition exists in the charter of goods.

External Debt. The debt held by persons outside a country.

Face Value. The value stated on the face of a security or insurance policy. This is the value on maturity or death.

Factor. A merchant who buys and sells on commission the goods if the bill drawn is not honoured.

Free on Board (F.O.B.). It means that the sale price covers all charges, including delivery of goods, free on board truck, car or vessel at a designated point, either at the origin or the destination of a shipment.

Free on Rail (F.O.R.). It means all expenses up to the loading of goods in rail will be borne by the seller.

Fraud. Securing consent to a contract by misrepresentation made with knowledge or by trick.

Goodwill. Value of a firm's reputation.

Gilt-edged Securities. Stock on which interest is safe.

Grace Period. Any period beyond the due date granted to a debtor by a creditor.

Gross Profit. Total allocable receipts of a period's operations less the cost of the goods sold, before allowing for operating expenses and income-tax.

Hire-purchase. A system for the purchase of goods, by which they are obtained on hire and each payment is also treated as a party payment of the purchases.

Hypothecation. It means pledging of goods or a ship.

Imports. Commodities or services brought from foreign countries.

Impost. A tax, particularly used to describe import duties.

Indemnity. Security damage or loss.

Indent. An indent is an order for the goods. In large store houses/ factories/workshops, etc., it is also used a requisition for stores.

Indorsee. One to whom an instrument is transferred by endorsement.

Indorser. Refers to one who has put his name on negotiable paper in order to transfer title (ownership) from himself to another or to guarantee payment.

Inland Bill. A bill of exchange drawn and payable within the country.

Insolvent. One who cannot pay debts.

Inter Alia. Among other things.

Interest. It is an amount paid on a loan or deposit. It is usually calculated at a certain rate per cent per annum.

(i) *Simple Interest.* This is paid only on the sum lent.

(ii) *Compound Interest.* This is paid on the sum lent plus simple interest till the time of payment.

Interest Bond. A bond issued in payment of interest on other bonds because of a shortage of cash to pay the interest.

Interim Bond. A temporary certificate which is replaced by a permanent bond at a later date.

Invalid Note. When a promissory note is obtained by misrepresentation or under threat or for illegal gratification such as gambling, bribery, etc. the note becomes invalid.

Invoice. A business form showing the items shipped and charges therefor sent by the seller at the time of shipment.

I.O.U. (abbreviation I owe you). It is an acknowledgement of a debt.

Jeruder. Customs official who searches ships for dutiable articles. He also checks ships, papers relating to import of goods.

Jettison. The throwing overboard a ship of goods etc. on account of bad weather or enemy action etc. The owner of the property is sacrificed, for the preservation of the whole, has a claim upon the owners of the property preserved, who are bound to share his loss with him.

Jury. A body of persons chosen and sworn to hear and pass verdict upon evidence brought forward in a trial, inquest or inquiry.

Legal Tender. Paper of metal money that a Government declares must be accepted as a lawful payment of debts.

Letter of Allotment. A letter informing an applicant for shares that certain shares have been allotted to him.

Letter of Credit. A letter written by one person to another, directing him to pay or hold a certain sum of money at the disposal of the third party. It is not transferable by endorsement.

Licence. It is a permission given to do some act, which, without such permission, would be unlawful.

Lien. A legal right of a person to detain or control property belonging to another until certain charges upon it have been paid or until some pecuniary claim against the owner has been satisfied.

Liquidation. The winding up affairs of an organisation.

List Price. The price shown in the sales list of the seller.

Liability. Debt or responsibility.

Long. The day-to-day record of a ship's voyage in the form of a diary.

Long Bills. Bills of exchange drawn payable at a period exceeding three days after date of sight.

Manifest. A list of goods on board a ship/aircraft.

Margin. A percentage deposited with a broker to secure him against loss by violent fluctuation of price.

Market Cheque. It is a cheque marked by the drawer banker guaranteeing for its being good for payment.

Market Area. That territory within which the product's purchase or sale affects the price generally prevailing for that commodity.

Market Price. The price at which the goods are exchanged in the market from day-to-day or current ruling price in the market.

Market Value. The price at which stocks, bonds, notes or goods sell in a given market at a given time.

Maturity Date. The date on which an obligation is due.

Maturity Value. The amount which must be paid on the date an obligation is due.

Memorandum of Association. It is a document which indicates the name, address, objects and powers, the limitation of members' liability and the share capital of the Company. It further defines the limits of the field of operations.

Merchandise. Goods.

Middleman. One who stands between the producer or manufacturer and the consumer.

Monopoly. Market situation in which one person or a group has such a control of the supply of a commodity as to be able to regulate its price.

Mortgage. A dead transferring property to a creditor as security for the payment of a debt.

Negotiate. To conduct business transactions, to pass cheque. To discount a bill of exchange.

Negotiable Instruments. Documents such as bills, notes, cheques, bonds etc. that by common usage on transfer by delivery from one person to another, convey a legal right to the property therein, free from all claims.

Net. The remainder after all deductions.

Net Profit. Profit after all deductions.

Net Sales. The total of all sales after deducting returned sales.

Normal Price. That price which will in the long run make the rate of production and rate of consumption equal.

Notary. A person duly authorised by the Government to take oaths, attest writings, etc.

Notarial Protest. The evidence required by law of the due presentation of a bill for acceptance or payment.

Obligation. Any enforceable debt (business). A duty owed by one person to another (legal).

Octroi. A tax imposed on articles coming inside a city. Revenues from such sources generally go to municipal bodies.

Official Exchange Rate. The ratio which is applied by the monetary authority of one country in exchange for that of another country.

Open Cheque. An uncrossed cheque payable on presentation to "bearer or order" as the case may be.

Open Credit. Credit given by a banker to customers without guarantee or security.

Open Indent. An importer's purchase order to an exporter, which may be filed with goods from any manufacturer or firm provided the goods meet specifications.

Opening Price. The price at which the first sale on an organised market is made on a particular day.

Open letter of Credit. A letter of credit without special conditions.

Open Rate. See *'Market rate'*.

Order. Verbal or written instructions for the purchase of goods.

Output. The quantity of goods produced in a given time.

Overdraft. A draft drawn in excess of the amount owed by the party upon whom the draft is drawn.

Overhead. All expenses except for those of the cost of raw materials, labour, sales, etc.

Owner's Risk. Railways convey goods at reduced charges at owner's risk. It means that the Railways are not responsible for any loss or damage except caused through misconduct of their servants.

Par. A stock or bond selling for exactly the amount expressed upon its face, is said to be at par. When selling at a profit, it is said to be at "Above Par" When selling at a loss, it is called "Below Par".

Par of Exchange. The value of a country's money in that of the other, comparing gold with gold and silver with silver.

Par Value. In the case of bonds and stocks, the face value appearing on the certificate is the par value.

Patents. A patent is an exclusive right granted under the Patents Act to the inventor of a new useful technical invention.

Patent Infringement. Unauthorised use, sale, or manufacture of a patented article.

Payee. The person named on a cheque, bill of exchange or other document, who is to receive payment.

Pay In. The deposit money in a bank.

Petty Cash. A cash or fund for small disbursements. It is also termed as petty fund.

Plaintiff. One who brings a suit in a court of law.

Pledge. It is a bailment of personal property by the owner to another as security for a debt.

Policy. In insurance, it is the contract between the insurer and the insured setting forth the various terms and conditions of the contract.

Pool. A combination formed to control the price of merchandise.

Post-dated. It pertains to a cheque or other document which bears a date subsequent to the date of delivery.

Power of attorney. A document authorising a person to act legally for another.

Pre-paying. Paying before the date on which payment is due.

Price. The amount of money which expresses exchange value of a single unit of goods, as 1000 grams, or 1 kilo of tea leaves.

Proforma. Latin for 'for the sake of form'. Used to describe in accounting, financial and other statements or conclusions based upon assumed or anticipated facts. A type of specimen.

Promissory Note. A written promise by a person to pay a specified amount on a specified date.

Pronote. Written promise to pay on demand or at a specified future time to a person specified or on his order.

Pro rata. In proportion to respective rights or liabilities.

Prospectus. Circular containing an outline of an article, commercial enterprise for public favour or comment.

Proviso. Conditional stipulation.

Quantity discount. A discount allowed on the principle that large quantities involve lower costs.

Quotation. The current published price of any commodity or security. Often two prices are given: — (1) the price asked for by the sellers; and (2) the price offered by the buyers.

Rate. The charge per unit for goods or services.

Rate War. Cut-throat competition between two or more carriers in an effort to attract freight by cutting rates.

Rebate. Part of payment returned.

Receipt. A written acknowledgement that something has been received.

Refund. To pay back.

Re-Insurance. Transfer of a part of risk from one insurer to another.

Remittance. Money sent by one person to another.

Representative. An agent or a salesman.

Return. The full account of business transactions.

Returns. The proceeds of business transaction.

Revocable Letter of Credit. A letter of credit which can be cancelled at any time.

Sabotage. Deliberate conduct damaging machinery, destroying raw materials, or turning out defective work.

Salvage. Property saved from a fire or a wreck.

Sealed Tender. A tender presented to an officer with seals, to be opened on the day fixed for the purpose.

Second of Exchange. The second copy of a bill of exchange marked "second".

Secured Creditor. A creditor who has collateral security in the form of personal or real property for a sum due to him.

Shareholder or Stockholder. The owner of a stock certificate, a part owner of the corporation.

Shipment. Articles put on board the ship for transportation.

Sight. Said of bills of exchange payable when received and in which no days of grace are allowed.

Sight Bill. A bill payable on sight, as soon as it is presented.

Sight Draft. A cheque or draft on bank, commercial house or debtor which demands payment immediately upon presentation.

Sleeping partnership. One in which only capital is furnished and no active part is taken in business.

Slump. A period of bad trade caused by lack of demand for commodities.

Solvency. The ability to discharge all debts and obligation in full.

Special Agent. An agent whose powers to act for his principal are limited.

Speciality. An article dealt in chiefly or exclusively.

Spot Price. The price for goods deliverable immediately.

Speculation. Selling of goods or securities in the hope of making a profit from the change in price.

Stock Exchange. A place where stocks and bonds are purchased and sold through brokers under definite rules and at regular hours

Syndicate. A combination of persons or firms to achieve a common business purpose.

Tariff. Is a protection for indigenous industry or measures undertaken by any country to protect its own industry against trade competition from outside.

Tax. A compulsory payment to the Government to defray the expenses which it has incurred in performing services for the common benefit.

Tender. An offer to buy or sell.

Terms. Conditions on which an agreement is made or on which a sale is made.

Time Bill. A bill of exchange payable at a future date rather than immediately.

Trade Bill. A bill of exchange drawn by the seller of the goods on the buyer covering payment of the goods.

Trade Discounts. These are the discounts allowed to the middlemen.

Trade Mark. A distinctive device or imprint used by a person or firm to identify his products.

Ultra Vires. Latin for "beyond the powers". Generally used to describe an act by a corporation or its agent which is beyond its powers to set out in the articles of incorporation.

Underwriter. Any person, banker, or syndicate that guarantees to furnish a definite sum of money by a definite date to a business or Government in return for an issue of bonds or stock.

Unilateral Contract. It is a contract that is binding on any one party to it, such as a loan of money.

Unsecured Creditor. A lender whose loan of debt is not secured by any collateral or mortgage.

Unship. Unload from a ship.

Usance. The customary number of days or months in which foreign bills of exchange are drawn in a certain place.

Vendor. Pedlar or hawker.

Venture. Business enterprise, especially of a speculative nature.

Warrant. A magistrate's order for the arrest of a person or seizure of goods; or a receipt for goods deposited in a warehouse and a negotiable document entitling the holder to certain money or property.

Wash. A fictitious sale or transaction.

Will. Legal disposition of property on one's death according to the written instructions of the deceased.

Writ. A written command in the name of State or Court directing the State or Court to act or abstain from acting in some way.

8
Common Prepositions

Given below is a list of prepositions commonly accepted as the standard in modern English :

A

Abide, *by*
absolve, *of* or *from*
abstain, *from*
absent, *from*
acceptable, *to*
accompanied, by, *with*
accede, *to*
accord, *with*, *to*
account, *for*
accountable, *to*, *for*
accrue, *to*
add, *to*
address, *to*
adjacent, *to*
advance, *of*, *in*,
advantageous, *to*
apologise, *to* (a person)
appeal, *to* (a person)
appeal, *for* (help)
appeal, *against* (sentence)
apprised, *of*
appropriate, *to*
apropos, *of*
appear, *to*
apply, *to* (a person)
apply, *for* (a thing)
adjudged, *to*
affixed, *to*
afflicted, with
agree, *to*, *with*, *upon*
agreeable, *to*
aim, *at*
allowance, *for*
allot, *to*
alternate, *with*
amalgamate, *with*
amount, *to*
answerable, *to* (a person)
answerable, *for* (conduct)
anxious, *for* (safety)
anxious, *about* (the result)
apologise, *for* (some fault)
arrange, *with* (someone)
aspire, *for* (fame)
aspire, *for* (fame)
ask, *for* (a thing)
ask, *of* or *from* (a person)
assured, *of*
astonished, *at*
assign, *to*
attend, *to*
attendance, *at* (a place)

appoint, *to* (a post)
approve, *of*
argue, *against, for* (person)
argue, *with* (some one)
argue, *on* (a subject)
arrange, *for* (something)
attendance, *on* (a person)
attacked, *with* (fever)
attacked, *by* (robbers)

attach, *to*
avail oneself, *of* (something)
answer, *to*

B

Bar, *to*
bargain, *with* (a person)
bargain, *for* (a thing)
based, *on* or *upon*
become, *of*
beg, *of* (a person)
beg, *to* (do a thing)
beg, *from* (somebody)
beg, *for* (something)
belong, *to*
believe, *in*
beneficial, *to*
benefit, *of*
beset, *with*
blame, *for*
blush, *at*
blessed, *with*
born, *into* (the world)
born, *of* (woman)
born, *to* (goodluck)
born, *in* (a country)
bound, *to*
burst, *into* (tears, anger)
break, *into* (a house)
break, oneself *of* (a habit)
break, *through* (bad news)
break, *with* (relating)

C

Capable, *of*
capacity, *for*
careful, *of* (money)
careful, *about* (dress)
cater, *to, for*
cause, *for* (anxiety)
cause, *of* (trouble)
caution, *against* (error)
catch, *at*
certain, *of*
centre, *on*
centered, *in*
characteristics, *of*
complain, *of*, *against*
concerned, *at*, *about*
concerned, *for* (welfare)
concerned, *in* (business)
concerned, *with* (a matter)
condemned, *to*
concentrate, *on*
concur, *with* (a person)
concur, *in* (a suggestion)
concede, *to*
concession, *to*
concurrence, *with*
concurrence, *in*

cheat, *of*
charged, *with* (crime)
charge, *for*
charge, *against*
clash, *with*
claim, *on*
claim, *against*
clamour, *for*
coalesce, *with, to*
co-equal, *with*
conincide, *with, in*
combine, *with*
copassion, *for*
compensation, *for*
committed, *to*
comparable, *to*
copy, *from*
cured, *of*
customary, *for*
correspondence, *with, to*
confine, *to* (a secret)
confine *in* (a person)
connect, *with*
connive, *at*
consent, to
conducive, *to*
confidence, *of*
confirm, *to*
congenial, *to*
congratulate, *on*
consistent, *with*
cosequent, *upon*
conspicuous, *for* (talents)
conspicuous, *by* (absence)
contingent, *upon*
contrast, *with*
contribution, *to* (a fund)
contribution, *towards*
convicted, *of*
co-partner, *with* (a person)
co-partner, *in* (something)
converse, *about* (a thing)
converse, *with* (a person)
convert, *to* (a faith)
convert, *into* (money)
correspond, *to* (agree)
correspond, *with* (write)
count, *for* (amount to)
count, *on* (rely)
cured, *of*

D

Deal, *in* (commodity)
deal, *with* (a person)
debit, *to*
defend, *against*, *from*
defraud, *of*
depend, *on, upon*
deprive, *of*
derive, *from*
desire, *of*
destined, *to, for*
disagree, *with* (a person)
disagree, *to* (a proposal)
disappointed, *of*
disappointed, *in*
disappointed, *with*
disapprove, *of*
dismiss, *from*
displaced, *with*
dispose, *of*
dissuade, *from*

detrimental, *to*
devoid, *of*
dictate, *to*
die, *of* (disease)
die, *from* (injury)
die, *by* (famine)
die, *for* (cause)
differ, *from* (to be unlike)
distrust, *of*
divide, *between* (two)
divide *among* (above two)
divide, *in* (half)
divide, *into* (parts)
doubtful, *of*
draw, *from*
differ, *with* (a person)

E

Eligible, *for*
emerge, *from*
empty *of*
endowed, *with*
engaged, *in, on* (business)
engaged, *to* (a person)
engaged, *with* (person)
engaged, *for* (responsibility)
enter, *into, on* (one's plans)
enter (a career)
entitle, *to*
entrust, *with*
equivalent, *of*
estimated, *at*
exchange, *for*
expelled, *from*
experience, *of* (a thing)
experience, *in* (something)
extort, *from*

F

Fall, *from* (estimation)
fall, *on* (attack)
fall, *in* (love)
fall, *into* (error)
fall, *upon* (evil days)
fall, *among* (thieves)
fall, *out* (quarrel)
fall, *to* (begin eating)
fall, *behind* (late)
fall, *back* (withdraw)
fall, *back upon* (depend)
fall, *off* (leaves, hair)
favourable, *to* (prospects)
favourable, *for* (action)
fearful, *of*
fight, *for*
fire, *on, at* (a man)
fire, *upon* (a mob)
forgetful, *of*
furnish, *to* (a person)

G

Get, *at* or *on* (acts)
get, *over* (recover)
get, *away from* (escape)
grieve, *at, over, about*
grieve (an event)
grieve, for (a person)

get, *out of* (debt)
get, *to* (a journey's end)
grateful, *for* (a thing)
grateful, *to* (a person)
guard, *from* (harm)
guard, *against (mistake)*

H

Hesitate, *to*
hide, *from*
honoured, *with*
hover, *over*
hunt, *after, for*

I

Identical, *with* (a thing)
illustrative, *of*
impatient, *at* (an event)
impatient, *of* (reproof)
impatient, *for* (results)
import, *into, from*
impose, *on*
incentive, *to*
include, *in*
inclusive, *of*
inconsistent, *in* (behaviour)
inconsistent, *with* (facts)
indebted, *to* (a person)
indebted, *for* (kindness)
indebted, *in* (money)
indispensable, *to*
inferior, *to*
influence, *over* or *with*
influence, *on* (action)
inimical, *to*
intent, *on*
interest, *in* (a thing)
interest, *with* (a person)
introduced, *to* (a person)
introduced, *into* (a place)
invasion, *of*
invited, *to*

J

Jealous, *of*
jump, *into* (well)
jump, *at* (accept)
jump, *to* (conclusion)

K

Known, *for* (his talents)
known, *by* (his name)
known, *to* (others)

L

Lapse, *into*
laugh, *at*
lay, *down* (arms)
lean, *against* (a wall)
lay, *before* (facts)
lay, (blame) *at*
lead, *to*
live, *on* (income)

lean, *on, upon* (a person)
lean, *to* (to be persuaded)
level, *with*
liable, *to* (mistake)
liable, *for* (payment)
liking, *for, to*
live, *in* (Delhi)
live, *for* (riches)
live, *at* (23, D.J.K. Road)
live, *by* (hard labour)
live, *within* (one's income)
live, *with* (the problem)
look, *after* (children)
look, *at* (a person, a thing)
look, *into* (examine)
look, *for* (search)
look, *through* (glance)
look, *to* (be careful)
look, *up* (be careful)

M

Make, *good* (fulfil)
make, *out* (draw up)
make, *over* (transfer ownership)
make, *for* (move toward)
margin, *for* (losses)
margin, *of* (mistake)
marked, *with*
match, *with, for*
merge, *into with*
mistaken, *for* (person)
mistaken, *in* (a belief)
mix, *in* (society)
mix, *with* (people)
moved, *by* (appeals)
moved, *with* (appeals)
moved, *with* (appeals)
moved, *with* (emotion)
moved, *at* (sight)

N

Need, *for*
negligent, *of* (duty)
negligent, *in* (work)
nomination, *of* (a person)
nomination, *to* (a post)

O

Obliged, *to* (a person)
obliged, *for* (something)
offend, *against*
offend, *with* (a person)
offend, *at* (something done)
opposed, *to*
overcome, *with* (fatigue)
overcome, *by* (entreaties)

P

Part, *with* (a thing)
part, *from* (a person)
participate, *with* (a person)
participate, *in* (a thing)
pledged, *to*
point, *to* (some result)
point, *at* (a person)
polite, *in* (manners)
polite, *to* (a person)

partnership, *in* (a thing)
partnership, *with* (a person)
pass, *away* (die)
pass, *by* (a place)
pass, *for* (a clever guy)
pass, *on* (transfer)
pass, *over* (comment)
pass, *off* (take place)
pass, *out* (consciousness)
pass, *through* (experience)
pay, *for*
persevere, *in*
persist, *in*
pertain, *to*
pity, *for*
play, *on* or *upon* (instrument)
play, *with* (treat lightly)
play, *up* (exaggerate)
play, *into* (the hands of)
play, *at* (play non-seriously)

Qualified, *for*
quarrel, *with* (somebody)

Reason, *with* (a person)
reason, *for*, *about*, *against* (something)
rebel, *against*
reconcile, *to* (a loss)
reconcile, *with* (a person)
recover, *from*
reduce, *to*
refer, *or*
regardful, *of*
regardless, *of*
regret, *for*

praise, *for*
predisposed, *to,* towards
prefix, *to*
prepare, *for* (the worse)
prepare, *again*st (disaster)
present, *with* (a thing)
present, *to* (a person)
preside, *over*
preside, *at*
prevail, *on*, *over*, *with*
previous, *to*
profit, *to* (a person)
profit, *by* (experience)
proof, *of* (guilt)
proof, against (temptation)
proud, *of*
provide, *against* (a rainy day)
provide, *for* (one's dependents)
provide, *with* (something)
purge, *of,* from

Q

quarrel, *over*, about (something)

R

rest, *on* (bed)
rest, *in* (a belief)
rest, *with*
result, *of* (consequence)
result, *from* (a cause)
result, *in* (a consequence)
retire, *from* (business)
retire, *to* (bed)
revert, *to*
rid, *of*
rival, *in* (anything)
rival, *for* (a position)

relevant, *to*
rely, *on*
remind, *of*
remonstrate, *with* (a person)
remonstrate, *against* (a thing)
remonstrate, *for* (action)
replace, *by*
replete, *with*
reply, *to*
request, *for*
resign, *from*
role, *of*
run, *after* (eagerly follow)
run, *into* (debt)
run, *over* (by vehicle)
run, *through* (waste)
rush, *against* (strike)
rush, *on* (attack)
rush, *at* (come forward)
rush, *into* (print)
rush, *out of* (house)
rush, *through* (work)

S

Scared, *to*
search, *for*, *after* (something)
search, *into* (look carefully)
secondary, *to*
see, *through* (understand)
see, *to* (attend)
send, *for*, to
serve, *in* (the army)
serve, *for* (an excuse)
serve, *with* (court summons)
set, *about* (begin working)
set, *down* (put down in writing)
set, *forth* (begin journey)
set, *in* (reaction)
set, *on* (fire)
set, *out* (journey)
set, *upon* (attack)
set, *to* (begin doing some thing)
set, *up* (start business)
set, *forward* (strange)
set, *off* (journey)
share, *of* (a thing)
secure, *from* (harm)
secure, *against* (attack)
see, *about* (consider)
see, *into* (investigate)
speak, *of* (a subject briefly)
speak, *on* (a subject in detail)
speculate, *in* (shares)
speculate, *or* (future)
stand, *against* (resist)
stand, *by* (support)
stand, *on* (one's prestige)
stand, *up* for (defend)
stand, *or reason* (logical)
stand, *down* (retire)
stand *for* (represent)
stand, *in* (share)
stand, *off* (remain aloof)
stand, *out* (conspicious)
stand, *to* (abide by)
stand, *up to* (face boldly)
stand, *on* (one's own feet)
strange, *to* (a person)
strange, *in* (appearance)
subject, *to*

share, *with* (a person)
side, *with* (a person)
side, *in* (a dispute)
similar, *to*
sin, *against*
slow, *of* (speech)
slow, *in* (deducing)
slow, *at* (accounts)
sorry, *for*
supply, *with* (a thing)
supply, *to* (a person)
susceptible, *of* (explanation)
subscribe, *to*
substitute, *for*
succeeded, *to* (a property)
succeeded, *in* (understanding)
sue, *for*
suffer, *from* (fever)
suffer, *for* (mistakes)
suited, *to* (an occasion)
suited, *for* (a post)
susceptible, *to* (influence)
sympathise, with (a person)
sympathise, *in* (troubles)

T

Take, *after* (resemble)
talk, *over* (discuss)
temptations, *to*
thankful, *for*
threaten, *with*
tired, *of* (doing anything)
tired, *with* (exertion)
touch, *at* (ships, a place)
touch, *upon* (brief reference)
trade, *with* (country)
trade, *in* (commodity)
translate, *into*
treat, *of* (a subject)
treat, *with* (respect)
treat, *to* (dinner)
triumph, *over*
trust, *in* (a person)
trust, *to* (someone's honesty)
trust, *with* (a thing)

U

United, *with*, *to*
urge, *on*, upon
used, *to*

V

Variance, *with*
vested, *in* (a person)
vested, *with* (powers)
vie, *with*
void, *of*
vote, *for, against*

W

Wait, *at* (table)
wait, *for* (a person, thing)
wait, *on* (attend a person)
weak, *of* (understanding)
want, *of*
warn, *of* (a danger)
warn, *against* (a person)
work, *at* (a task)

weak, *in* (his head)
weary, *of*
wedded, *to*
witness, *to*
work, *for* (money)
work, *upon* (feeling)
worthy, *of*
wrestle, *with*

Y

Year, *for,* towards
yield, *to*

Z

Zealous, *for* (improvement)
Zealous, *in* (a cause)
zest, *for*

9
Advertisements

Advertisement plays a vital role in modern business. Someone has rightly said: "Advertisement to business is what medicine is to a patient".

There are thousand and one media and forms of advertisements. In fact, the subject is so vast than even a complete book would not be sufficient. We have therefore, selected a few forms of advertisements which appear in day-to-day news papers and magazines and on signboards etc.

Advertising a Birth

Leslie Howard and Mrs. Clara joyfully announce arrival of first grandson, Son to Maj. Rupert and Gloria, grandson to Mrs. Sarah Dawson of Liverpool on Thursday, 8th April.

An Engagement

Sticks-Richardson—Hector, son of Mrs. Anglela and Mr. Michael Hicks to Lawra, daughter of Mrs. Lolla and Mr. George Richardson, Grant Road, on 9th March.

A Marriage

Marian, daughter of Mr. & Mrs. Wilson weds Victor on 4th January at Hilton Hotel, New Jersey, at 9.00 p.m.

A Death

Samuel, son of Nicholas Host, 14 Bretton Road, expired suddenly on 5th June.

Accommodation Available

Available on Rent, Three-Room Flat, fully furnished ground floor, Hewilt Road, London. Ring 3643721 between 2 and 5 p.m. on working days.

Accommodation Wanted

Wanted a Four Room independent bungalow for the General Manager of an American Company. Willing to pay up to $800 per month. Agreement in the name of the Company. Apply immediately, Box No. —, New Statesman.

Sale of a car

Self driven Rover, 25,000 k.m. Show-room condition. Must sell today. Ring 4444446.

Business Offer

Wanted Stockists in all big cities for our latest 'J.K. Pimple Cream'. Write with full details to J.K. Pimple Cream Private Limited, IPOH (Malaysia).

Business Wanted

Spacious Show Room with telephone at Metro Cinema, Singapore. Wanted agencies/representation/liaison/business proposal. Write Jang, Metro Cinema, Singapore.

Situation Vacant

Wanted Fast Typist with minimum speed of 50 words per minute. Apply stating full particulars regarding qualifications, age, experience, salary drawn and salary expected, to National Traders, Colombo.

Situation Wanted

Wanted Accounts work on contract, Ring 5283271.

Advertising a Senior Management Appointment: Wanted

WORKS MANAGER

For a lager Engineering/Electronics complex to be established in the suburbs of Yangon.

Candidates must have good degree in Engineering, at least ten years Production/Planning experience in this trade. Minimum age 30 years. Those drawing less than US $1000 per month are unlikely to be considered.

Applicants should apply to Box 1403, "The Myanmar Express", Yangon, and must include bio-data. Full details of working career and also precise salary and conditions expected. Applications which do not include all the above particulars will be rejected summarily.

This position is with an old established public limited business house and will provide the successful applicant with good career prospects. Applications must be submitted before 15th September.

Hotel Facilities

HOTEL HIGHLAND
Glasgow

Air-conditioned, central location, swimming pool, Bar, Channel music, independent telephone, attractive tariff and special arrangement for conferences and parties.

Telephone	Gram
235876 (14 lines)	*Comfort*
Fax	
235919	

Competitive Exams

Special Sessions start from 1st and 15th May for Defence and Civil Services Examinations.

Hostel Facilities available.

NIP COLLEGE OF COMPETITIONS

10, D.N. Road	Wales
Phone:	14371
Principal	M. Collins

(M.A. Econ., M.A. English, M.Ed.)

Tool and Alloy Steel

Available Ready Stock of Everything in TOOL and ALLOY STEEL. High Speed, Carbon, Stainless, Oil Hardening, High Carbon, Hot Die, Silver-Nickel Chrome, etc.

Write for details:

SIMSON TOOL COMPANY
10, Mound Road, Bristol
Phones: 184326 & 184327

Safety Blade

More & More People Choose
SHARPEDGE
for smoother Shaves

Clearance Sale of Shoes

Ladies, Gents & Children Shoes
SIMPLE SHOES
Discount upto 15% for Ten Days
DIMPLE SHOE COMPANY
Connaught Road, New Jersey

Fresh Arrivals

Terene Suitings
Terry/Cot Suitings
Terry/Cot Shirtings
Printed Dress Material
Cotton Print Dresses
and
Silk Dresses
FASHION HIGH
14-Esplanade, Mexico City

Available for Disposal

Two Nos. each imported holdings and closing line motor brake unit ad 3 and ad 2 respectively for Morrison, Australian make over-head crane, Drawing available on request. Interested parties may contact.

Stores Officer
Yangtse Cement Limited
Kowloon
Hong Kong.

Tender Notice

Managing Director, Mexico State Small Industries Corporation, invites sealed tenders from well-established Contractors in the execution in interior decoration work for the interior work of Mexic an Government Emporium, Jerico Road, up to 1.00 P.M. on 24th Nov. The tenders will be opened at 2.00 P.M. on the same day in the Mexican Govt. Emporium, Jerico Road, Mexico City.

Tender forms can be had from the Sales Manager, Mexican Govt. Emporium, Mexico City from Sept. 13 to 17, and should be submitted to him along with earnest money deposit of US $1000 in the form of a Bank Draft in the name of Mexco State Small Industries Corporation, Mexico City.

Government Auction

GOVERNMENT AUCTION

Under the orders of Tax Recovery Officer (Income Tax), X, London, House Property No. 16, Bentik Street, London, will be sold by public auction on Wednesday, the 14th March, at 4.30 P.M. on account of realisation of income tax dues from Paul Rover, Bentik Street, London. The auction will take place at the said property itself. The highest bidder will have to deposit 25% of the price at the fall of hammer by cash or by Bank Draft and the balance within two months. For their terms, please contact:

M/S. LIFTON AND COMPANY

Bentik Street, London

Phone: 582037

State Lottery

NOW EMIRATE LOTTERY

Offers

First Prize of **Dir. 5,00,000**

(common to all series)

2 Second Prize

Dir. 1,00,000 each plus Free Air Ticket for 2 round Europe or Dir. 35,000.

5 THIRD Prizes
Dir 25,000 each
50 Fourth Prizes
Dir 2000 Date of Draw 13-10—
and 5982 other prizes

Directorate of U.A.E. Lottery.

Opening a new branch of the bank

CENTRAL BANK
EXPANDS
MOUNT ROAD BRANCH
Opened at
Rusa Buildings
Mount Road, London
On 31st December

Earn Interest

Earn 9% to 15%
ON FIXED DEPOSITS
with Public Limited Companies

For details contact:—

SAMUEL BROS.
Haridasa Street
Colombo.

An Exhibition

Freedom Struggle and the Legislature
AN EXHIBITION
Parliament House, Room No. 63, First Floor
Open to the public today
11 a.m. to 6 p.m.
Organised by the Exhibition Division of the D.A.V.P.
Minsitry of I.&B.

V.P. Bargains

Outstanding Books

Selected Letters	US$	8.00
Business Letters	"	8.00
Encyclopedia of G.K.	"	20.00
I.A.S. General Studies	"	50.00
Railway Service Commission	"	15.00
Top Party Jokes	"	10.00
3,000 Quotations	"	8.00
3,000 Idioms	"	8.00
3,000 Proverbs	"	8.00
3,000 Synonyms and Antonyms	"	8.00
Grammar and Composition	"	8.00

Packing and Postage Extra

Mail orders to:—

GOODWILL PUBLISHING HOUSE
B-9, Rattan Jyoti, 18 Rajendra Place,
New Delhi-8
(INDIA)

Appeal Regarding Advertisement

ALLIED PRODUCTS EMPLOYEES' ASSOCIATION
SYDNEY

Shri. N.M. Jackson
President of the
Reception Committee,
M/s. New Light Industries,
Sydney-2023.

March 8, 19........

Gentlemen,

I am pleased to inform you that the Cultural Division of the Allied Products Employees' Association has decided to stage sometime in May a full-length drama of topical interest, DERAILED, written by a well-known dramatist.

This is the first venture undertaken by our Employees' Association and hence deserves your co-operation and full support.

To coincide with this occasion the Employees' Association has decided to bring out a Souvenir which will comprise interesting articles for distribution among the patrons and sympathisers to publicise the occasion.

I shall be grateful to you for lending your generous support to this maiden venture in general and through advertisement to this Souvenir in particular. Finance is the life-blood for successful execution of any venture. Therefore, taking a suitable advertisement space by you in the Souvenir will mean a real help to foster the noble aspirations of the Association. This small support may enliven the occasion and set in motion the creative impulse that has manifested now among the Employees' Association of our Industry.

Thanking you,

Yours faithfully,

Sd/-

Encl: Advertisement Tariff

N.M. JACKSON
President
Reception Committee

Advertisement Tariff

ALLIED PRODUCTS EMPLOYEES' ASSOCIATION
SYDNEY

Ref. : Advt.

Date: 8-3-19........

M/s. New Light Industries,
Sidney.

Dear Sirs,

The Cultural Division of our Association is going to stage a Drama entitled "DERAILED" and a Physical Show by Mr. Robert Wells and his party shortly.

We, therefore, request you to kindly co-operate with us for the success of the function by booking an advertisement space in the "Souvenir" going to be published on the occasion. The advertisement rates are detailed below. Please fill in the form and send it to us by 7th April, 19.....

Thanking you, Sir.

Very truly yours,
Sd/-
Secretary.
Allied Products
Employees' Association

Advertisment Rates and Mechanical Data

Inside full Front Cover	US$	10	
Outside full Back Cover	"	150	
Inside full Back Cover	"	90	20 cm x 20 cm.
Inside full page	"	70	
Inside special position full page	"	60	
Inside half page	"	55	20 cm x 9 cm
Inside quarter page	"	40	9 cm x 9 cm

Overall size of the Souvenir 2 cm x 24 cm

FORM

To
The Secretary,
Allied Products Employees' Association,
(Cultural Division),
Sydney.

Dear Sir,

In response to your letter No. ____________ dated ____________ I/We request you to kindly book one outside full back cover/Inside full front cover/Inside full back cover/Inside full/Inside half/Inside quarter/Inside special page of advertisement space for us in your "Souvenir" to be published on the occasion of staging the drama "DERAILED" at the rate of US$ ____________ (Dollars ____________ only).

The matter/block and the cheque are enclosed.

Encloures: As above

Yours faithfully,
Signature with Seal

Cheques should be drawn in favour of "Allied Products Employees' Association" A/c. Payee only.

Enclosing advertisement matter

May 26, 19.....

Advertisement Manager,
Melbourne High School,
London-7.

Dear Sir,

We enclose herewith one page advertisement matter which may please be inserted in the earliest available issue of 'High School Annual'.

Thank you,

Yours faithfully,
for NEW MODE PUBLISHERS

Encl: Advertisement matter.

Reply to the above

Telephones: 9351461, 951562
Telegrams: Bhavidya

MELBOURNE HIGH SCHOOL
North High,
Melbourne,

May 29, 19........

BJ/AD/2167/73
M.s. New Mode Publishers,
West Avenue,
Melbourne.

Dear Sirs,

Re: **Yours advtg. in HIGH SCHOOL ANNUAL**

With reference to your letter No. N/20/721 dated 26-5-19...... we confirm that your full page advertisement will be published in Bhawan's Journal issue dated 11-6... in a prominent position.

The cost of this advertisement is US $250 plus 14% surcharge and our bill in this connection will be sent to you in due course along with necessary vouchers.

Thanking you,

Yours faithfully,
Sd/-
Secretary School Annual

Asking a client to subscribe for a magazine

THE NEW WAVE DIGEST

(A Journal of the Publishing and Bookselling Industry in England)

NLD: Subs. 43, Crest Road,
17th, March 19...... London.

M/s. National Book Company,
Scotland.

Dear Sirs,

You must have come across **The New Wave Digest** somewhere during its ten years of existence. This journal reaches every publisher, bookseller, wholesaler, librarian and even individual book-lovers.

It has 6904 subscribers on its mailing list from all over England and abroad and is one of the best media to publicise books. In continuous publication since 1954, this journal has been catering to the book-trade in a number of ways. Our special features are current News from the Book World Reviews, Notes and News, Persons and Places, Events, etc. Besides, it discusses all the important problems that the trade is facing today and it also lists titles in English and other European languages which are published during the last three months for which we claim to be pioneers.

The annual subscription is only £50 and in case you are not yet a subscriber, please send in your subscription today. We would be glad to send the specimen copies for your perusal.

The Subscription Form is enclosed.

Yours faithfully,
(D.N. Roger)
Advertisement Manager

Encl: Subscription form.

Requesting to condense a portion of publication

Tel. No. 43
Gram: C.C. College

OXFORD COLLEGE STUDENTS' UNION
Oxford South, England
Motto: CLARIOR TENEBRIS

Ref. No. CC/SU/Mag/71-72/10 Date: 11-4-19.......

To

New Lead Publishers,
Royal Place,
Kuala Lumpur.

Subject: Prayer of permission to condense a portion from your Publication.

Sir,

May I please lay the following few lines to you for favour of your permission.

That the Oxford College, the only College is going to publish the fourth volume of its annual Magazine. The manuscripts also will be given to the press for publishing within this week.

And that, we like to include in it one Article reading 'He Marches to Immortality' condensed from your esteemed publication 'Martin Luther King, Martyr for Freedom' by M.K. Alexander. The condensed article is also attached for your kind perusal and correction.

I, the secretary to the Magazine Department in the College Students' Union, therefore, sincerely pray for your permission to include in the publication the condensed article to enrich our Magazine, to popularise your publication and to spread and emphasize Freedom of Equality.

I hope my prayer will receive your kind acquiescence.

Yours faithfully
Sd/-
(Bon Kings)
Secretary,
Magazine Department,
Students' Union.

Reply to above

April 21, 19......

The Secretary,
Magazine Department,
Oxford College Students' Union,
Oxford South,
England.

Dear Sir,

We thank you for your letter No. CC/SU/Mag/71-72/10, dated the 11th instant.

We have no objection to your including the article on Martin Luther King in your Magazine.

Please send us a copy of your Magazine, when published.

Thank you,

Yours faithfully,
for NEW LEAD PUBLISHERS
Sd/-
Partner

10
Circulars

Announcing Sale

15th March, 19........

Madam,

We beg to advise you that our Annual Stock Clearance Sale will start on 21st March, and will be open till 7.30 p.m. on 31st March.

This time, the prices have been heavily reduced—as much as 50% on certain items.

The sale consists of a wide range of Cotton and Silk gowns, Towels and Bed sheets; Dunlop Pillows and Pillow Covers; Ready Made Garments for men, women and children; Handkerchiefs and Underwears; Ties; Caps; Mattresses, etc.

We hope you will be able to pay us a visit and make your selections. On the other hand, if you feel, you will not be able to come personally during the sale period, we are enclosing our catalogue and shall be glad to reserve any goods up to the amount of our stocks. Any such order should be accompanied by full payment in advance.

Assuring you of our best attention and awaiting your order.

We are, Madam,

Yours faithfully,
For Fancy Wear Stores

Goods Supply

NATIONAL RESEARCH INDUSTRIES,
Hoyle Road, Kentucky
MEDICAL CIRCULAR

You will be pleased to learn that our research laboratory has synthesized a new food-cum-medicine Vitamin X, which has been found very useful in the cure of diabetes.

A bottle of 50 tablets costs US $20.00 and we offer ten per cent discount to the trade.

Only an early order will help us to meet your demand.

Yours faithfully,

Sd/-

Sale of Residential Plots

SALE OF RESIDENTIAL PLOTS

IN SECTOR-8, Colorado

Colarado, the most modern and beautiful city planned for a population of 77,000,000 in another two years, offer the most harmonious and please living environment.

Salient Features of Sector-8

Abutting Sector 7, a fully developed and mostly built up sector.

★ Hardly a mile from Town park and Town centre.

★ Picturesque site overlooking the airport and abutting the proposed by-pass.

★ Freehold, full ownership

★ Relief from local taxes for a long time.

★ No annual lease money.

★ Planning on most modern lines with wide landscaped roads, underground sewerage, drainage, water supply, modern shopping centre and public amenities conveniently located.

★ No restriction on owning more than one plot.

Plots of 134 Sq. mts., 210 Sq. mets. and 300 Sq. mts. are being offered for sale US $150 to US $200 per sq. mt. Those paying full price in lump-sum with the application will get Big Concession in price and also the choice to select plot on the spot on the basis of "First Come First Served". Sale will continue up to 30th March.

Application forms with layout and full information can be obtained on payment of US $1.00 in cash or by sending US $1.0 by Money-order from the Administrator, Urban Estate, Sector 12, Colorado (Tel. 22988, 23334), or Liaison Officer, Lytton Road, Colorado (Tel. 385933, 386131/42).

Director, Urban Estates, Colorado

Announcing Change of Manager

December 21, 19.......

Dear Sirs,

We write to advise you that Mr. A.M. Hafeez relinquished his appointment as Manager on the 20th of this month when he left our employment. He has, therefore, no authority to act for us in any respect from that date.

Mr. Salim Ahmed has been appointed our new manager with effect from today.

Your faithfully,
For Mohammad Bros.
Sd/-
Managing Director

Offering Services for Repair of T.V. sets.

H.V. T.V. & ELECTRONICS

Television Servicing and Repairs Centre,
Kingston Road, Tel: 382763
London. Date: ....

Dear Sir/Madam,

We feel privileged in introducing ourselves to you as Television Engineers with about 10 years' experience in T.V. Manufacturing/Servicing.

We wish you a happy T.V. viewing but should you need our help, we shall be pleased to put our services at your disposal very promptly and at reasonable charges. As the repairs are undertaken under the supervision of a Glasgow trained Electronics Engineer, we assure you of a convenient and excellent look-after of your T.V. receiver set. You may also ask for the terms of our "Annual Servicing Contract" Scheme.

Yours faithfully,
For H.V. T.V. Electronics
Sd/-
Derrick
Partner

Wednesday Closed

Offering Translation Services

INTERLINGO

18, Rajendra Place, New Delhi (INDIA)

Tel.: 5761729, 5761820 Fax: 5768040

Dear Sir,

We have the pleasure to introduce you to our Organisation, INTERLINGO, that undertakes translation work in all languages (INDIAN OR FOREIGN).

The nature of work may be technical, medical, scientific, cultural or literary, we do all the translation promptly and accurately.

There are over fifty hands, all accurate in translation work in different languages, on our panel.

Additionally, the salient features of our Organisation are:

THOROUGH execution of assignment on schedule.

Charges VERY FAIR

Cover the main languages of the world.

Undertake TRANSLATION OF ALL KINDS, not excluding technical or scientific side. Even manuscripts are taken special care of.

We earnestly hope that you will give us a trial to convince you of the utility of our services to your esteemed organisation.

Awaiting earliest response with your valued patronage.

Thanking you,

Yours faithfully,

For INTERLINGO

Sd/-

Director

Circular Regarding Advertising

INDONESIA TIMES

JAKARTA

March 18, 19....

Dear Sir,

25 years of Progress in the South

We have the pleasure in announcing the publication of a Special Supplement on "25 years of Progress in West Indonesia" with our issue, dated 10th April 19....

This will be a bumber supplement with separate sections dealing with development programmes and the progress achieved in the Region and in various field of activity such as industrial development, food and agriculture, power generation and rural electrification, transport and tourism, housing, banking, etc. The supplement will carry interviews, articles and special contribution from leaders and specialists in their respective fields of activity.

Rates of advertisement in the supplement will be as usual and the rate applicable to advertisers already holding contracts with us will be as per subsisting contracts. Advertisers not holding contracts will be charged at our currently applicable rates which are given below:

Casual US $2.00 per *s.c.* cm. (inclusive of 10% surcharge)

Contract (300 cms. and over) .... US $1.50 per *s.c.* cm. (inclusive of 10% surcharge)

Closing date for advertisements in one week before the date of publication but it will be appreciated if your release order and material could be sent to us as much in advance as possible.

We are sure, you would like to take space in the supplement and we look forward to receiving your release order and material at an early date.

Thanking you,

Yours faithfully,
For Indonesia Times
Advertisement Manager

Establishment of New Business

ROYAL STORES
Hasan Abel Road,
Cairo (Egypt).
Tel.: 52216, 52217 Fax: 52117

12th August, 19....

Gentlemen,

We have pleasure in informing you that construction of our new departmental store at the above address, is now almost completed and it shall start functioning from 20th August, 19____.

Fully air-conditioned with most modern amenities, the store has been under charge of Mr. Mohammad Siraju who had been our branch manager for the last 20 years. Mr. Siraju has an excellent experience in departmental store line and it will assist us in selecting the best goods and in running the business on the most efficient lines. In fact, whenever we have opened a new branch in any city, we have always appointed Mr. Siraju its incharge for at least five years.

'All-in-one' — We shall store all things of daily requirements—General Merchandise, Cloth, Soaps, Watches, Cycles, Books, Toys, Games, etc. We have adequate capital at our disposal and we hope to make our store as big as in Rome, London and Paris.

Will the quality of the goods offered will always be the best, the prices will be reasonable on account of our bulk purchasing.

When you come down to Hasan Abel Road next time for a cup of coffee or otherwise, just drop in for a moment and see what we say.

We are confident of receiving your patronage.

Yours faithfully.
Royal Stores

Announcing a New Publication

Goodwill Publishing House
18, Royal Place,
California.
20th July, 19....

Messrs ....
....
....

Dear Sirs,

We have pleasure in informing you that our new book entitled, "1001 Jokes" is now available in the market.

Printed on white paper with 200 pages, the book is priced US $10.00 only.

It has been complied by Shri C. Lincoln, compiler of 'Lovers Jokes'—a book which has fetched tremendous sale during the last few months. We have already received quite a large number of bulk order. We are sending separately under book-post a title of the book which speaks of itself.

Ours terms of sale are:—

1 to 50 copies 33% F.O.R.
51 to 100 copies 35% F.O.R.
101 to 200 copies 37½% F.O.R.
200 copies and above 40% F.O.R.

Payment:— R/R through bank.

We may add here that our next book. "Applications for Better Jobs"—by Dr. J.D. Johnson, M.A., Ph. D, Author of 'Model Letters'—will be out on 13th May and we shall send you the title within two/three days.

We now await your order which will receive our most careful and prompt attention.

Thanking you,

Yours faithfully,
for Goodwill Publishing House.
Sd/-

Wanted
DISTRIBUTORS
For Our
ELECTRONIC EQUIPMENT

We make a wide range of industrial electronic equipment, control system and panels of vital use in industry. Each item is precision engineered to fit the job and the process. The range includes:

Time Delay Relays & Sequence Timers, Liquid Level Controllers/ Indicators and Pump Control Panels, Single Phasing Preventor with low and high voltage protection device, Automatic Lighting Controllers, Mercury switches, Electronic Flash Tubes, Hydro Welders A.C. & D.C.Tacho Generators & Proximity Switches, Road Traffic Signalling Equipment, Automatic Diesel Engine Starting Equipment, Multipoint Temperature Monitoring Panels, Alarm Annunciator Panel, Digital Preset Counters, Digital Clock, Under Frequency Relays and other equipment.

Make a future in Electronics—

As a distributor of our fast-selling electronic equipment, you should have well-trained sales engineers and live-wire salesmen with experience in this line; a showroom for display and demonstration; excellent contacts with government and industry; intimate knowledge of the market in your area. Above all, you must be willing to invest well in these speciality products. If you measure up to these requirements, this lucrative distributorship is yours. Please, therefore, write to us within 10 days with full particulars and your bank references.

Volkart Electronics Pvt. Ltd. London

Retiring from Business

KOWLOON SPORTS
Kowloon,
Hong Kong.

16th Nov, 19........

Dear Sirs,

As I am now getting on in years, I have decided to retire from business from 30th Nov. 19....

I have disposed of all my machinery and raw materials to M/s Sanyet & Co. They have also taken some manufactured stock. I am now left with a manufactured stock of £50,000 only. I wish to sell it by lots against cash. Since you have always been one of my very good customers, I suggest that you pay me a visit as early as you can and make me an offer for the particular stock you may be interested in.

I will always remember with feelings of pleasure the friendly relations we had for the last so many years and I sincerely wish you a continued and increasing prosperity.

I remain
Yours faithfully,
Sd/-
T. Yang

Taking over a Business

20th Nov., 19____

Dear Sirs,

We write to inform you that on the retirement of Mr. Yang, proprietor of Kowloon Sports, we have taken over the entire business conducted by him.

We propose to trade under the same title and maintain the firm's reputation of top quality, courteous attention, moderate prices and prompt execution of orders.

We further with to add that effective 16th of this month, we have appointed Mr. Nelson George our new Technical Director. Mr. George is a States trained personnel and has worked in an American firm for the last 15 years.

We thus feel we shall be able to serve you to your entire satisfaction.

Excepting your best co-operation,

We remain,
Yours faithfully,
Sd/-
Sanyet & Co.

Announcing Admission of a New Partner

HARRIS & CO.
Dolls Manufacturer,
London

16th Jan. 19____

Dear Sirs,

In view of large increase in my business, I have this day taken into partnership Mr. B. Richardson and henceforth my business will be run under the name and style of:

HARRIS, RICHARDSON & CO.

Mr. Richardson was Manager in DOLLS INTERNATIONAL, Tokyo, for the last eight years and has, therefore, adequate experience about this trade.

Mr. Richardson also brings a cash investment of £50,000 and I hope we shall be able to expand our business to the extent of marketing our products in areas which remained untouched owing to restricted production.

I am grateful to you for your past patronage and hope for a continuance of the same.

I remain,
Yours faithfully,
Ian Harris

Sending a Catalogue

14th Oct. 19____

Dear Sirs,

We have pleasure in introducing ourselves as one of the largest publishers of General Books in India with 350 titles to our credit.

Our books are being widely circulated throughout the world.

Regular advertisements appear in top magazines and daily papers of countries and our clients are *harvesting* heavy profits on keeping bulk stock of our publications.

While on the one hand our books are most moderately priced, on the other and more important, we exchange all non-selling books with our other publications.

We hope you would also be interested in keeping stock of our publications and with this end in view, we enclose a latest copy of our catalogue.

Yours faithfully,
For World Publishers
Sd/-

Encl. Catalogue

Education/Employment Abroad

Persons desirous of seeking Employment or Higher Education in U.S.A. or Canada may contact.

OVERSEAS EMPLOYMENT COMPANY

3954, Wood Street, Erle, Pennsylvania, U.S.A. (16509) for information about job opportunities, introduction to employers, schools and travel plans, On receipt of a short resume of qualifications and a self-addressed air mail envelope (23 x 10 cms), the applicant will be provided with necessary information, etc.

Note. Replies will be sent by Air Mail on receipt of 5 International Reply Coupons available at all post offices. Enquiries accompanied with International Reply Coupons will receive their replies by Sea Mail in the course of 5-6 weeks.

Invitation to an Exhibition

Witness all the exciting recent developments in fibres, yarns and fabrics at

THE 'FIBRES AND FABRICS OF TODAY AND TOMORROW' EXHIBITION

Inauguration by

Governor of Chicago, Mr. Stnart Low, at 5 P.M. today.

Venue : The Institute for Industrial Research, 19, University Road, Chicago.

Duration : 23rd March to 1st April on all week days between 4.30 P.M. and 10 P.M and on holidays between 3.30 P.M. and 11 P.M.

Sponsored by : Ministry of Foreign Trade, United States, Director of Industries, Chicago;
National Research Development Corporation, United States; Northern America Cotton Textile Mills' Association; Chicago Manufacturers' Organisation, Chicago State Board; and Institute for Industrial Research, Chicago.

Admission Free

Free transport to and from the Exhibition available every hour from 16.00-21.00 hours.

Auction of Surplus Stores

GRAND AUCTION

Surplus U.K. Government Stores

Airconditioners — Refrigerators — Gas Cookers, Typewriters, Recording Machine — Adding Machine — Slide Projectors — Garrard Turn Tables — Chromium Reflectors — Spot Lights — Exhibition Materials — Carpets — Office and Household Furniture and Miscellaneous Items.

On Sunday, 25th march, 19 — at 10 a.m.

at the British High Commission Compound

London

Terms: Cash and Carry on as is where is basis, no warranty to working or effectiveness.

On view: 8.30 to 9.30 a.m.

Auctioneers: CAPITAL ENTERPRISES, London.

Fresh Arrivals

JUST UNPACKED

Superb designs for this year's summer

* ORGANZA, in style prints!
* COTTON GEORGETTE For all occasions
* KOTA PRINTS in artistic designs!
* CHIFFON PRINTS in unusual designs!
* CHINON PRINTED in new styles!
* SILK PRINTED Kashmir & South Indian!
* ORGANDIE PRINTS!
* VOILS and several others!

CONTINENTAL GARMENTS

Readymade Garments Store *(Fully Air-Conditioned),*

40, Down Street, London.

Phones: 66330, 65892.

Job-Oriented Course

JOB-ORIENTED COURSES

There being an urgent need for candidates trained in Computer Sciences and Programming, CICS offers Comprehensive course in Computer Science preparing them to take up jobs. Most of the CICS trainees have secured remunerative jobs easily in leading concerns.

Admissions are open for the following courses:

Computer Science:

Post Graduate Diploma course—one year—covering Electronic Data Processing, Types of Computers, Storage Media, Programming Languages, PERT/CPM etc.

Fees: US $2,000 (inclusive of course material). Commencing 4th April, 19...

Television Technology:

TV technicians have excellent job opportunities throughout the country. CICS offers a comprehensive course with practical training under expert hands. Many CICS trainees have found jobs with STANDARD TV, TELEVISTA, WESTON, TELERAD and some of them have set up workshops.

Duration: 4 months (part time) Fees: US $300 p.m. Commencing 8th April 19...

Fortran IV Programming:

Duration: 2 months (part time): fees: US $750. Commencing 14th March 19...

Autocoder Programming :

Duration: 2 months (full-time) Fees: US $850 Commencing 4th April, 19...

COMPUTER INFORMATION COURSES & SERVICES

208 Elgin Road, London 3128.

Telephone: 42989

Packaging Machine

SUPER INDUSTRIAL & TRADING CO.,

Our Ref. 87/73

10th Sept., 19..

Dear Sirs,

Sub: Shrink Packaging Machine

We have pleasure in introducing ourselves as manufacturers of Shrink Packaging Machines indigenously developed by us.

As you are possibly aware, Shrink Packaging has acquired tremendous importance all over the world, in as much as it provides the following advantages:

1. *Lower shipping costs.*
2. *Eliminates costly dunnage.*
3. *Produces stronger Package through unitization.*
4. *Saves money on packing materials and storage space.*

5. *Produces plastic package that are unaffected by moisture and dust barrier.*
6. *Displays merchandise immediately.*
7. *Simplifies identification and inspection.*

Both shrink tunnels and low density Polyethylene shrink films are available indigenously. Shrink tunnels do not require very high investments and the maintenance expenditure is also negligible. 'SUPER' shrink tunnels are also made to suit customers' requirements. Major features of our 'SUPER' tunnels are given in the attached bulletin.

Shrink packaging is suitable for almost all products such as textiles, cosmetics, pharmaceuticals, *stationery, paper, products,* plastic wares, engineering goods, food products, miscellaneous items such as crockery, glass wares, containers, toys, garments, tins and innumerable consuming articles.

We would be most pleased to shrink pack certain items of your interest for demonstration and satisfaction.

For more details, please refer to the enclosed literature on Shrink Wrapping Machine.

Should you have any doubts, please feel free to write to us.

Thanking you,

Yours faithfully,
For SUPER Industrial & Trading Co.,
Sd/- Manager

Encl: Literature on Shrink Wrapping Machine.

Educational Circular

Dear Sirs,

NATIONAL BOOK FAIR

Supplement of February 4.

The National Book Trust will hold the Fifth National Book Fair in Hong Kong from Jan. 25 to Feb. 4. To mark this important event and to serve the Book Trade, Hong Kong Gazette—will bring out a supplement in its issue of Feb. 4 which will be on sale on Feb. 1.

Hong Kong Gazette with a circulation of 2 million copies per issue spread over the entire English-speaking World, is very popular with lovers of books and book trade. The supplement previously brought out on "Book Trade" last year and "World Book Fair" year before last were much appreciated by all concerned.

The supplement will carry interesting and informative articles on all aspects of Book Trade by experts. We are sure, you would participate in it by release of your advertisement. Last date for receipt of instructions, material and payment is Jan. 10.

The advertisement tariff is given below:—

Casual	*Contract*
per page	per page
per. s.col. cm.	per s.col. cm.

Yours faithfully,
For J.D. Coleman & Co. Ltd.,
Sd/-
Advertisement Manager (Dev.)

Commercial advertisement

ANSON & ANSON ASSOCIATES
Picadilly, London
ESTATE AGENTS & CONTRACTORS

Off: 3721
Phones:
Res: 563201

Ref. No.: 83/73

Date 14th April, 19____

Re: Showrooms, Shops & Offices on Ownership/Rental Basis.

Dear Sir,

We most pleasantly inform and offer, being the Selling Agents, shops and offices on instalment basis in King's Plaza Complex and Royal Estate, George's Avenue, London. Most of the traders and professionals are purchasing shops and offices there. The booking is very fast. These are the best propositions as these complexes will develop better than having Cinema

Halls, private offices and shopping centres with big walk-ways connecting all the buildings having sufficient parking space. We shall be pleased to furnish you with further details, if asked for.

We shall appreciate if you book it early to avoid non-availability of the best bargains.

We can also arrange Office accommodation, Flats, Shops and Godowns and rent as well as ownership basis is and around Picadilly Circus and other Commercial Areas.

Thanking You,

Yours truly,
For Anson & Anson Associates
Sd/-

11

Applications and Appointments

ESSENTIALS OF A GOOD APPLICATION

1. Always use good paper for application. White bond-paper is considered to be the best one for this purpose.

2. Write application yourself.

3. Use only one side of the paper.

4. Address application correctly—Do not confuse Post Box No. with 'Newspaper' Box No.

5. Type application neatly.

6. Give proper margins. Normally there should be more margin at the bottom than on the top.

7. Arrange paragraphs systematically.

8. If you are already working, never use the letter-head of that firm for writing an application.

9. The application should be so written that it stimulates enough interest and curiosity and creates a desire in the mind of the employer to see you personally.

10. The application should induce a feeling of goodwill and friendliness in the prospective employer.

11. Write respectfully and modestly but frankly, stating your qualifications without boasting or under-rating.

12. Application should be correct and tidy. There should be no mistakes concerning elements of grammar, spellings and punctuations.

13. Do not include any such thing in the application as may tantamount to the creation of an unfavourable reaction.

14. Your application should vindicate your personality distinctly and should be specific and to the point. It should not apply to any other person who may have similar qualifications and experience.

15. Be brief, but do not leave facts at the cost of brevity.

16. Use headings, capital letters and underline important words and phrases to highlight your application.

17. Show your confidence in being able to handle the job efficiently.

18. Give your reasons for your desire to leave your present position, if you are currently employed, wherever necessary.

19. Send application according to requirements of the employer—thus—where an application is required in handwritten form, a type application should never be sent and *vice versa*.

20. Use good envelope for the application. As far as possible the envelope should be uniform with the application paper.

21. Submit an application immediately on publication of the advertisement.

22. State when and where the advertisement appeared.

23. Apply for every job for which you possess minimum qualifications required and where you may be interested, even remotely.

24. NEVER USE CARBON COPIES.

25. Whenever a call is received, prepare yourself for appearing in the interview even if you may not be finally interested in that job. Every interview adds to your experience and you receive some useful information which might help you in getting a good job subsequently.

26. Where the advertiser does not give his address, i.e., invites applications c/o Box No.... of a 'NEWSPAPER' always address your application to the Advertiser, and not to any other person.

27. Application should not be sent under Book-Post cover.

28. Avoid using postcard for writing applications.

29. Do not apply for jobs for which you do not possess specific qualifications.

30. Do not send application under registered cover care of Box No. of a newspaper.

STRUCTURE OF AN APPLICATION

An application consists of the following parts:—

1. The address of the writer.
2. The date of writing the application.
3. The name and address of the employer.
4. The salutation.
5. The introductory or opening paragraph.
6. The body of the application.

7. The concluding paragraph.
8. The subscription.
9. The signature.

1. Address of the Writer

An application beings with the address of the writer and by far this is the most important part as the reply would be received only if the address is correct. It is, therefore, necessary for the writer to place his address in a conspicuous position so that the reader may be able to see to it easily. The usual form of writing the address is—top right-hand corner. However, where an application is written on the prescribed form of the employer, it should be written only at the proper place provided for the same—and not necessarily on the top right-hand corner. Similarly, where the application is written in the serial or bio-data form, the address should be written under its proper heading only.

2. Date of the Application

It is always desirable to put correct date on the application. The date should normally be written below the address on the top right-hand corner, such as,

311 Harrison Street
London 3110/1A
Date:

unless otherwise specified in the prescribed form of the employer.

3. Name and Address of the Employer

The name and address of the employer is equally important. This should generally be written above the salutation. Clear discrimination must be made in 'Post Box No.' and 'Newspaper Box No.' such as

(*a*) The Advertiser,
Post Box No. 811,
Grand P.O.
London.

(*b*) The Advertiser,
4 Strait Times
Box No. 16970,
Singapore.

4. Salutation

Proper selection of the salutation is necessary. Distinction must, be made between "Sir" and "Dear Sir". Sir is more formal than, "Dear Sir" and as such it is always desirable to use "Sir" while addressing the applications to Government or Public Officials. In case of applications addressed to head of business firms, it is always better to use 'Dear Sir'. Salutation should appear two/three lines below the name and address of the employer, like:—

(*a*) Estate Officer,
Ministry of Urban Development,
New York.

(*b*) The Advertiser,
"The Bangkok News"
Box No. 1697,
Bangkok.

Dear Sir:

The address to which an application is required to be addressed in case of Government jobs, is generally mentioned in the Advertisement and where the address is care of (c/o) 'Newspaper' only, the salutation should be "Dear Sir".

5. Introductory or Opening Paragraph

Much depends on your opening sentence. Your first sentence expresses your sense of writing application and your general intelligence. It should, therefore, be brilliant, convincing and striking. Remember: "Well begun is half done".

Wherever possible, you can use such brilliant sentences like:—

For the post of Salesman:— "Wait. Don't put down this letter. If you do, you will miss the chance of a life-time to hire a crack salesman".

For the post of a Hotel Manager:—"They licked their plates clean! I know this for two reasons. Firstly taste tell me. Secondly like the people in the fairy tale, my customers lick their plates clean!"

While in general the opening paragraph is meant to contain a statement of the applicant's desire to be considered for the post, it can be expressed simply and directly, such as

(*a*) I wish to apply for the post of "Stenographer" in your firm, advertised in today's "Daily Times".

(*b*) In response to your Advertisement in this morning's "The Tribune", I submit my application for the above mentioned post (mention the post against subject:—Post of Scientific Assistant) in the light of my qualifications and experience given below.

(*c*) In reply to your advertisement in today's "New Statesman", I request to be considered for the post of a 'Senior Clerk' in your firm and as desired by you I give below a short description of my qualifications, age, experience, etc.

(*d*) Understanding that you require the services of an Accounts Clerk in your Company, I wish to apply for the post. Please keep in view the following facts:

(*e*) Having heard from one of my friends in your service that you need an 'Accounts Clerk' in your office, I offer my services for the post and hope that you will give me an opportunity of proving my worth in due course of time.

(*f*) With reference to your advertisement in "The Morning News" dated 17th July, 19..., for the post of 'Stenographer', I have the honour to offer myself as a candidate for the same and submit the following for your kind consideration:

(*g*) I wish to be considered a candidate for the post of a 'Traffic Manager', which, I understand, has fallen vacant in your office, recently.

(*h*) Having seen your Advertisement for an 'Accountant' in today's "The Leader", I offer my services for the vacancy. I give below particulars regarding my qualifications, experience, etc., and hope that you will give me an appointment at a time most convenient to you when I may call at your office for an interview.

(*i*) I have been informed that you require the services of an experienced travelling salesman for your goods. I, therefore, take this opportunity of placing before you the following particulars regarding my qualifications, experience, age, etc. I hope you will appoint me your travelling salesman for Sydney and Melbourne.

(*j*) I understand that there are a few vacancies of teachers in The Secondary School, Manila. I feel honoured to apply for one of them.

(*k*) With reference to your Advertisement in the "Free Press" dated the 6th of August, 1973, I beg to apply for the post of a General Clerk—an opportunity that I have just been looking for, because only yesterday my services were terminated in the Thompson's

Stores, as I was the last hand to be employed and the management wanted to economise a little during the usually slack monsoon season.

(*l*) Reliably given to understand that you need some reporters for your Paris Branch, I hasten to offer you my services for such an assignment in your Paris Editorial office.

(*m*) Your advertisement for a paint salesman emphasizes your need for a thoroughly competent person with merchandising education and practical experience. Will you take a moment to consider my qualifications?

(*n*) Five years' experience as a Stenographer in the personnel department of a large industrial firm qualifies me, I believe, for a similar position with your firm.

(*o*) Is there a need in your firm at this time for a Secretary with several years of experience in the automotive field?

6. Body of the Application

Here a brief account of age, qualifications, experience, etc. is to be given. The applicant should try to convince the employer about his suitability for the post. Mention may also be made of a reference whom the employer, if he so desires, may contact to find out about the conduct and suitability of the candidate for the post.

While writing this part of the application, the applicant should realise that his fitness or otherwise for the job would depend upon his age, qualifications and experience and as such these particulars must be carefully drafted and then written—read and re-read to avoid mistakes of any kind.

(*a*) *Age:* Write only approximate age and not exact age in terms of years, months and days. Thus if the date of birth is 31st July, 1949, and the date of sending application is 28th October, 1988, the age should be written as 39 years or even 39 years and not 39 years, 3 months and 29 days.

(*b*) *Education:* Degrees closely related to the job advertised should appear first and prominently. Where the job lays emphasis on some special background and mere mentioning of the degree will not give adequate clarification, then subjects studied for the Degree should also be listed, *e.g.,* for the Medical Representative's post, emphasis is placed on scientific background. Supposing you are an

M.A. and had studied Science subjects for your Bachelor's degree, then you should list you qualifications as under:

Education:— (a) Bachelor of Science (B.Sc)

Subjects:— Botany
Chemistry
Zoology
English

(b) M.A. Economics

(*c*) *Experience:* The present employer is generally interested in knowing what you have done recently. It is therefore, desirable to write the details of your experience in the reverse order. You need not write your record in a chronological order unless your feel it useful. If your most important position had been prior to the last one, start with that. Similarly, if your experience at some previous job is better fitted to the advertised job requirements, put more emphasis on it.

Following information, if brief, should be mentioned regarding experience:—

(*i*) Name and address of Firm/Company employed in.
(*ii*) Designation held.
(*iii*) Important duties and responsibilities.
(*iv*) Any special achievements.
(*v*) Actual dates of employment.
(*vi*) Details of last salaries drawn (where necessary).

Reasons of termination of service or resignation should in general be ignored altogether. However, where necessary, they may be presented as "Firm closed business in the country due to import restrictions"; "Resigned for Better Prospects"; "Company closed its business on completion of some particular venture" etc.,

(*d*) *Seminar and special training courses:* State here brief details of postal tuitions, courses attended, seminars attended and certificates obtained, if any.

(*e*) *Prizes and merit scholarships:* Give a brief account of prizes won—for debates, sports, article writing, etc.—and scholarships granted by schools, employers, etc.

(*f*) *Extra-curricular Activities:* In this column of the application, give details of activities like Membership/Presidentship/Secretaryship of any Society, College Union, etc.

(*g*) *Journals and Magazines:* Mention here different journals and magazines to which you subscribe and which you read.

(*h*) *Registration:* Certain professions, *e.g.*, doctors etc. need registration. In such cases, it is always desirable to mention this fact.

(*i*) *Association Membership:* Membership of Associations like that of Institute of Cost and Works Accountants, Institute of Engineers, Medical Association, etc. should be specified clearly.

(*j*) *Hobbies:* Mention of hobbies is generally not necessary. However, where the hobbies have some relationship with the job, the same may be mentioned in brief.

(*k*) *Travel:* Taste for travelling and different areas where you have already travelled may be mentioned with advantage, where required.

(*l*) *Reference:* References and testimonials are important because they express the opinion of others about the applicant's suitability for a position. Therefore, where the applicant has got some previous experience, he should give references of personal friends.

Two or three references are generally sufficient. Hence where the applicant has several references to choose from, his choice should fall on the best-known among them. The fact that he can refer to well-known persons in his application, gives him an advantage over those who mention less-known references. It is advisable to secure permission from the references before mentioning their names in the application.

(*m*) *Salary:* As a general rule do not mention anything about present earnings or salary expectation since there is always a danger of one's being dropped out if that differs from the wishes of the employer. Even where the advertisement of the employer asks for mentioning salary expectations, it is sufficient to state that the matter can be discussed to mutual satisfaction during personal interview.

(*n*) *Photograph:* For certain jobs e.g., salesman, receptionist, Air Hostess etc., photograph is generally asked for by the Advertiser to judge the personality of the candidate before calling him/her for an interview. Latest passport-size photograph, in all such cases, should be affixed on the application. Candidate himself, on the own accord, should generally avoid spending any photographs unless he feels that such a photograph will indicate his exceptional personality.

(*o*) A mention may also be made about the following factors, where necessary:—

(*i*) Interest in going on tour.

(*ii*) Willingness for serving anywhere in the country.

(*iii*) Knowledge of foreign languages.

(*iv*) Owning and driving a car, motorcycle or bicycle, etc.

7. Concluding Paragraph

The concluding paragraph of the application is as important as the opening or the introductory paragraph. Here, an assurance is generally given by the applicant that he would do his best to give entire satisfaction to the employer in case he is selected for the job. A request for an interview is also made in this paragraph. A few examples of closing paragraphs are given below:

(*a*) I shall do my best to please my seniors with honest and hard work, if selected for the post.

(*b*) I shall be highly obliged if you could consider me for the post.

(*c*) I beg to assure you that I shall do my utmost to please you with my hard and honest work.

(*d*) Should you be pleased to give me a chance, I assure you, Sir, that I will do my best to satisfy you in every way.

(*e*) Hoping for a favourable reply.

(*f*) I trust you will grant me the favour of an interview.

(*g*) I shall be glad to be favoured with an interview.

(*h*) In view of the facts mentioned above, I hope you will not deny me the chance to prove that I possess the requisite taste and spirit for teaching. I am just asking for a chance to be of use of my country and the nation.

(*i*) Should you please call me for an interview, I shall be glad to give you any further information you may require.

(*j*) I shall look forward eagerly to hearing from you.

(*k*) I hope you will not disappoint me and give me a chance to fulfil the ambition of my life.

(*l*) Should I be fortunate enough to be selected for the post, I would use my best endeavours to merit your confidence by hard work and devotion to duty.

(*m*) An interview will assure you that I can fill this post to your complete satisfaction.

(*n*) I shall be able to call for an interview at your convenience and shall be delighted to supply any necessary references or examples of my previous work.

(*o*) I hope my application will receive your favourable consideration and that you will select me for an interview.

(*p*) Although I am almost fresh from school, I am anxious to do my best in any kind of work that may be entrusted to me.

(*q*) I sincerely hope that you will let me have a reply at an early date so that I may call at your office for an interview.

(*r*) If you will give me an appointment, I shall be glad to see you at your office and discuss the matter with you. I am prepared to take up any responsible position in your office and can assure you of efficient and intelligent service at all times.

8. Subscription

The subscription should agree with the salutation. Thus in case of letters addressed to the Government or public officials, the usual subscription for the higher positions should be:—

I have the honour to remain,
Sir,
Yours most obediently

....

While for lower positions, the appropriate salutation should be:—

I beg to remain,
Sir,
Yours most obediently

....

In case of commercial firms, "Yours faithfully" or "Yours respectfully", "Yours truly" or Yours sincerely,

9. Signature

In the case of a typewritten application, the handwriting of the applicant will be judged from his/her signature only and as such special care must be taken in writing it as legibly as possible.

In the case of a female, the applicant should clearly state by writing the word Miss or Mrs. in brackets before her signature, *e.g.* (Miss) Anita Sales (Mrs.) Mary Jefferson.

TYPES OF APPLICATION

All letters or applications may be divided into two categories namely:—(1) Solicited and (2) Unsolicited and an applicant seeking for a job may use one or both of them.

1. Solicited Application

A solicited letter of an application is one which is generally written in response to an Advertisement from the employer.

Following are a few examples of Advertisements from the employers:

"Accounts Officer on 700-50—2000, knowledge of Income-tax an asset, Registered Accountant preferred. Apply Victor Garments Manufacturing Company, Grant Road, Kuala Lumpur.

"Wanted experienced part-time stenographer any time between 10 a.m. and 5 p.m. for two hours. Apply with full particulars, copies of testimonials and minimum salary expected to Box 211, 'The New Times, Colombo'.

"Wanted for a well-established concern, Accounts Assistant, preferably a Graduate in Commerce with at least five years' experience. Apply with copies of testimonials, stating minimum salary expected to Box 2673, 'The Cairo News" Cairo.

"Large Foreign Shipping Corporation requires shipping assistant. Please apply in confidence giving full details, salary requirements, etc. to Box 2113, 'Antara News', Jakarta, Indonesia."

"Wanted Experienced Sales Representatives to book orders for consumer products. Please apply Box 22210, 'The Express,' London."

"Wanted Urgently for a Reputed French-medium school part-time/full-time Mathematics/Science teachers for higher classes. School hours 10 a.m. to 5 p.m. Higher pay according to experience. Phone 266435 or apply Box 14567, Algiers Times' Algiers.

The main advantage of such an application is that the applicant becomes sure about the existence of such a vacancy with the employer. Besides, since the requirements of the employer regarding qualifications, experience, age, etc. of the candidate are also given in the advertisement, it becomes easy for the applicant to apply only for the jobs to which his/her particulars will suit.

There is, however one main disadvantage of such an application and that is that since the vacancy is advertised, there is always a rush of applications with the employers and hence the application of any applicant would be one of many such applications, written in response to the advertisement. The applicant should, therefore, try to present his application in a manner that is better than an average application—rather he should try to make it one of the best applications received by the employer.

2. Unsolicited Application

An unsolicited letter of application is for a job which has not been advertised by the prospective employer.

This type of application has definitely one big advantage—the application does not stand to that big competition to which an advertised job's application is open. Besides, the applicant can send similar applications to the number of employers at the same time.

There are, however, two disadvantages also:— (1) It is possible that there may be no post existing with the employer at all; and (2) the writer must determine for himself the qualifications in which the employer will be most interested.

Following are a few examples a various types of applications:

Application for the post of a junior clerk

13-M.G. Road,
London 2031
7th March, 19____

The Advertiser,
Box 1444,
"The Mail",
London.

Sir,

I wish to apply for the post of a Junior Clerk advertised in "The Mail" of the 15th instant.

I am 22 years old and have just passed the Commercial Diploma Examination of Boston. I have also taken a course in Shorthand and hold a "Pitman's Shorthand Certificate" for 150 words a minute. My typing speed is 50 words a minute.

I enclose a copy of the Commercial Diploma and a testimonial from the Principal, College of Commerce, Boston relating to my character and proficiency in studies.

If I am appointed to the post, I assure you that I shall try my best to give you entire satisfaction.

Yours respectfully,
Jack Kramer

Application for the post of typist

14, Hilton Road,
London.
January 19, 19.........

Leads Wvg. & Mfg. Co.,
Leads,
U.K.

Gentlemen,

Your Advertisement for a 'Typist' in today's "The Sunday Times" emphasizes your need for a thoroughly competent person with sufficient practical experience. Will you take a moment to consider my qualifications?

I am at present 25 years of age and have got a sound physique and active habits.

It was in 19.... when I graduated from the Canton University in Commerce getting 70% marks in Accountancy and Auditing which I had offered as my special subject. During my college days only, I picked up typing at a private institute and my present speed is 60 words per minute. While in college one of our professor of English often used to give me his manuscripts which I used to type with great accuracy and obtained sufficient practical experience in typing even before my graduation.

Immediately after my leaving college, Mr. John Mills, a well-known Advocate of the High Court Canton, employed me on part time basis to type his legal documents. Along with it I was doing typing work of a commercial firm which involved a good deal of figure work.

The opinion which has often been expressed about my work fills me with confidence that I can turn out clean, attractive and well-spaced copies. A practical test will convince you of my as a typist.

It should also go to my credit as a typist clerk that I have dealt with the of a very delicate nature and kept it completely confidential.

I assure you that I shall do my best to give you entire satisfaction and hope to win your faith very soon.

Yours faithfully,
Jame Nigal

Application for the post of an Overseer

43, Abdul Street,
Dhaka.
November 13, 19____

The Proprietor,
Metal Corpn.,
Dhaka.

Subject: Post of Overseer, advertised in "Mornings News" dated 12th November, 19 ____

Dear Sir,

With reference to the above, I beg to submit the following details for your kind consideration:

Name : Karim Ahmed
Age : 24 years
Nationality : Bangladeshi
Education : Examinations passed with class obtained:

(*i*) Matriculation from the Chittagong University in 19____ with high First Class.

(*ii*) Diploma in Engineering from Hewitt Engineering School, Dhaka, in 19___, with Second Position in School.

Extra-curricular:

(*i*) One among Cricket Eleven in School Team.

(*ii*) Secretary, Dramatic Society of the School.

Testimonial and references:

I attach a testimonial from the Headmaster of High School and a testimonial from the Principal, Hewitt School.

I hope my application will receive your favourable consideration and that you will select me for an interview.

Yours faithfully,
Karim Ahmed

Application for Accounts Assistant

216, Grand Road,
Canberra
24th Sept., 19____

The Advertiser,
Post Box No. 1959,
Main P.O. Canberra

Subject—Your Advertisement in today's "Australia News" for the post of an 'Accounts Assistant'.

Sir,

With reference to the above I submit below full particulars of my age, qualifications, experience, etc:

Name : John Kelly
Age : 29 years

Educational qualifications:

(*i*) School final from Melbourne Board of Education in the year 19____ with high Second Class.

(*ii*) National Diploma in Commerce from Sydney University, with Advanced Accountancy (87% and Auditing 72%) as my special subjects. The aggregate percentage of marks was 68. Passed in 19____ .

(*iii*) Graduation (Commerce) from University of Melbourne in the year 19____ with high Second Class.

Apprenticeship:

Having passed my Diploma Course, I was sent to the Bank of Sydney for one year's training. The training was arranged by Sydney University in consultation with Bank of Sydney.

I had the opportunity to work in almost all the departments of the Bank, particularly: Receipt (Bill), Payments (Bills), Drafts, Correspondence and Records.

I was being paid a monthly stipend of US $200.

Experience:

(*i*) *Jr. Accounts Assistant* — In Pan Air Lines Corporation, Australia. The main duties assigned were Costing and Posting of—Goods Received Notes, Stores Issue Requisitions, Stores Transfer Notes,

Goods Returned Notes and Inventory of Stock with Ledger Accounts. I worked there for a period of one year and was being paid a monthly salary of US $800.

(*ii*) *Accounts Assistant* — For the last 5 years I have been working as an Accounts Assistant in one of the prominent semi-Government concerns. The main duties assigned to me are: Checking and Passing of Bills (Stationery and Printing, Trunk-Call and Telephone, Electricity, Sale of Books and Magazines etc.) for payment; Making out yearly budgets, Posting and maintaining of Different Accounts Registers and Ledgers and Independent Correspondence about the Accounts matters.

The present salary drawn is US $900 per month.

Sports and Games:

I was one among the Cricket X1 in my college and a very good player of Volleyball.

Extra-Curricular Activities:

I was President of my College Association and I am Secretary of Chit Fund Society in my present employment.

References:

Mr. ...... City Council
Mr. ...... Magistrate.
My Present Employers.

Present salary and other benefits drawn:

(*i*) Salary US $900 per month.
(*ii*) Social Security at 8½%.
(*iii*) Free Medical Facilities for all members of the Family.

Expected salary: US $1200 per month.

Notice Period: One month.

A copy of the photograph is attached herewith, along with other certificates and testimonials, as desired.

I am confident that you will find the above details suitable for the post advertised by you and shall kindly grant me an interview to give you any further information which you might like to have.

Yours faithfully,
John Kelly

Enclosures— Seven.

Application for post of a Purchase Officer

29, Chemsford Street,
London.
13th July, 19____

The Chief Engineer,
British Airways,
Lloyds Street,
London.

Dear Sir,

I have the honour to apply for the post of a 'Purchase Officer', advertised in yesterday's 'Sunday Telegraph', and give below particulars of my age, qualifications and experience:

Age — Thirty-one
Native Town — Bristol
Nationality — British

Education:

Examinations passed with classes obtained: —

(*i*) Matriculation from the London University, in the first class, in 19____ .

(*ii*) Junior Commerce from Bristol University, in the first class, in 19____ .

(*iii*) Senior commerce from Bristol University, in the first class, in 19____ .

(*iv*) Graduate in Commerce from London University, in the second class, in 19____ .

Extra-Curricular:

(*i*) Captain — College Cricket Eleven

(*ii*) Captain — College Volleyball.

(*iii*) Secretary College Union — Under Graduate

(*iv*) Secretary — College Debate Club — Graduate

(*v*) President — College Union — Graduate

Experience:

(*i*) 19____ 19____, Purchase Assistant, Delta Antibiotics, Melbourne.

(*ii*) 19____ to date, Promoted as Assistant Purchase Officer, Delta Antibiotics, Melbourne. Experience in this Organisation comprises calling of quotations, making of comparative statements, personal verification of articles placing of orders after consulting the Managing Director, checking of Inspection Notes and looking after all correspondence on the subject of 'Purchases'. Full familiarity with different forms used from purchases and stores like : Goods Received Notes, Orders Stores Issue Notes, Stores Transfer Notes, etc.

Testimonials and References:

(*i*) I attach a copy of the testimonial from the Dean, Faculty of Commerce, University of London, about my proficiency in studies and character.

(*ii*) As I am forwarding this application through my present employers, you may refer to my Managing Director regarding my work as Assistant Purchase Officer.

Salary Expected:

My present pay is US $750 and I expected an initial salary of US $1500 in the grade advertised.

Yours faithfully,
Johnson

Application for Part-time tutor (Part-time teacher)

42, S.M. Road,
London
10, 19____

The Advertiser,
"The London Times",
Box 1998,
London.

Dear Sir,

With reference to your advertisement in "The London Times", dated the 9th September, 19____, I have the honour to apply for the post of a Part-time Tutor, an opportunity that I have just been looking for because only yesterday I felt one of my private tuitions as the father of my pupil has been transferred to London and they are shifting to that place today.

Since I migrated to London after 19____, I am teaching the Higher Secondary School students of S.M. Higher Secondary School — English, G.K. and taking up Mathematics periods in the absence of Mathematics Teacher. I am generally having part-time tuitions (only two or three) up to Higher Secondary Standard — in English, Mathematics, G.K.

I am at present 49 years of age and have in all about 30 years of teaching experience. A great majority of my pupils have shown excellent results and occupy some of the topmost jobs in private and Government Offices. My way of teaching has always been more of a friendly nature than that of an instructor and my students have always liked me and tried to learn — being removed from the usual fear and treat of a teacher.

I can spare time between 8 p.m. and 9.30 p.m. and I expect a minimum tution fee of $200 per month.

I shall be glad to call on you at time convenient to you.

Yours faithfully,
R.N. Devaker

Letter of an Interview

A.B.C. & Co.
Hongkong
7th Sept., 19____

Ref......................
220, East Park Road,
Hongkong.

Subject—Post of a Clerk

Dear Sir,

With reference to your application dated 18th August on the subject cited above, please present yourself for personal interview before our representative, Mr. Hack Tuly, at Hotel Hilton, Hongkong on 15th September at 2.30 p.m.

Please bring with you the original certificate and testimonials at the time of interview.

No travelling allowance will be payable for appearing for an interview but, if selected, one day allowance will be paid for joining your duties at our Kowloon Office.

If selected, you will have to join immediately.

Please intimate by return of post if the terms mentioned are acceptable to you.

Yours faithfully,
For A.B.C. & Co.
Chung Jae Hock
Managing Director.

Letter accepting the offer

220, East Port Road,
Hongkong.

Date: 26th Sept., 19____

The Managing Director,
A.B.C. & Co.,
Hongkong.

Sir,

I am very much thankful to you for your letter dated 18th September, 19____

I shall report for duty on the 4th October at your Kowloon Office.

Thank you.

Yours faithfully,
San Ye Peng

Letter of Appointment

ABC & CO.,
Hongkong.

Dated: 28th Sept., 19____

Ref.
San Yen Peng
220, East Port Road,
Hongkong.

Dear Sir,

With further reference to your interview with our we have pleasure in offering you the Post of a Steno-typist on the following terms and conditions:—

1. You will be entitled to draw an initial salary US $500 of plus usual allowances as admissible under the Company's rules.

2. Your appointment at the first place is for 6 months but if the work is found satisfactory, you will be taken on the permanent roll of the Company.

3. During the period of first 6 months your services can be terminated at a notice of one day and likewise you may also give us one day's notice if you want to leave us but after confirmation of your service either party will have the right to do so at one month's notice.

4. You will be entitled to contribute to our Social Security Fund at the rate of 8¼% of your basic play to which the Company shall also contribute an equal share. The liability of the Company's share of contribution will arise only if you complete a minimum service of three years. Besides, total contribution, you will also be entitled to an interest at the prevailing bank rate, from time to time.

5. You will be entitled to bonus as declared by the Company for time to time (for the last five years a three months' basic pay has been given every year as bonus to each employee).

6. You will be entitled to 10 days, casual leave and 28 days' earned leave in a year.

7. Your appointment will be subject to being declared fit by the Senior Medical Officer of this Company.

8. If you accept the offer on the above terms and conditions, you may intimate to us by return of post and resume your duties at our above address before 4th October, 19____.

You may purchase a Second Class railway ticket for which the amount will be reimbursed by the Company.

Yours faithfully,
For ABC & Co.,
Chung Joe Hock
Managing Director

Resignation from an employee

11th January, 19____

The Secretary,
Colombo Productivity Council,
Colombo.

Sir,

For certain unavoidable circumstances of my family, it has become necessary for me to discontinue with my present service. I, therefore, request that I may kindly be relieved of my present duties as soon as possible, in any case not later than the 8th February, 19____.

My accounts in full may please be settled before that date.

Thank you.

Yours faithfully,
M. Richard,
Accountant

Negative Reply to the Application

A.B.C. & Co.,
Hongkong.

10th Dec., 19____

Mr. Sin Peng
Hongkong.

Dear Sir,

In reply to your letter about an appointment, we regret to inform you that we are unable to meet your wishes as the posts suitable to your qualifications were filled last month only.

Yours faithfully,
For ABC & Co.,
Chung Jae Hock
Managing Director.

Recommending an employee

WILKSON ENGINEERING WORKS
Esplanade Tower,
London.

16th July, 19____

Dear Sir,

Mr. Taylor, bearer of this letter, has served in this concern as an independent Accountant for the last five years and has now left us; as he wishes to settle in your town. He tells me that you are willing to offer him a similar post on my recommendation and it is with the greatest pleasure that I comply with his request. He is sincere, honest and hardworking and will always prove to be an asset where he works.

Yours faithfully,
For Wilkson Engineering Works,
Sd/-

Dismissing a Clerk

ABDULLA TRADERS
Kuala Lumpur.

18th Nov., 19____

Mr. Abid Hasan,
Commercial Department.

We have already had an occasion to express our dissatisfaction with your work and served you with a warning letter on 16th September this year. We hoped that the letter of warning would have impressed upon you the serious consequences likely to follow in the absence of your improving the work, but we regret very much to say that you have totally ignored the warning letter. We now feel it necessary to say that we cannot permit any of our staff members to continue here in an irresponsible way and since you are not a willing worker, we can no longer retain you in our employment. Please, therefore, accept this letter as one month's notice from date for terminating your services from this organisation.

Yours faithfully,
Sd/-

Testimonial from employer

TO WHOM IT MAY CONCERN

Certified that Mr. Victor Jones was employed as an Assistant Manager in this concern from 19____ to 19____.

During the course of his employment with us, we found him honest, sincere and hardworking.

Mr. Victor Jones would be a very valuable asset indeed for any concern and we would be pleased to recommend him for a responsible post.

We had to dispense with his services, as we are closing our business in Pakistan and shifting to America.

R. Wilson,
Managing Director,
XYZ Co.

12

Agency Distributorship

Enquiring about the Distributorship of Books

HARDFORD BOOK COMPANY
Norton Road,
New Jersey.

18th Nov., 19____

M/s. Simson Publishing House,
Rockefeller Complex,
New York.

Dear Sirs,

Re: **Distributorship**

We are very pleased to inform you that we are one of the leading distributors of books to wholesalers, retailers, schools, colleges and libraries and at present apart from our own publications, we are also the sole selling agents of National Lithographic Press (a division of National Tobacco Co. Ltd.) for eastern region of USA.

We are confident that we will be able to give you good business provided you appoint us your sole distributors. This is just for your information that our sales net-work is very active.

We hope you will not mind to reply by return of post quoting your terms and conditions, etc. On hearing from you, we will revert to the matter again.

Yours faithfully,
For Hardford Book Co.
Sd/- (Partner)

Offering distributorship of Books

BOOK TRADERS
California.

SIMSON PUBLISHING HOUSE,
Rockefeller Complex,
New York.

May 11th, 19____

Dear Mr. Bevin,

I take this opportunity of recalling the little acquaintance we had during the Publishing Managers Course at Hotel Royal.

We have now decided to add Library books to our Publishing programme from time to time and our first book entitled THE LEGENDS (Five Cantos) by Mr. William Maxmueller M.A., is being released on the 25th May, 19____.

As the book falls very much within the sale scope of your organisation, I hope you would be interested in bulk purchase of the same.

I am enclosing the circulars giving details regarding the book. These circulars can be got printed with your address if you so desire, at our expense.

I shall be glad to have a line in reply in the matter.

With best wishes and kindest regards,

Yours sincerely,
For Book Traders
(Robert Nelson)
Managing Partner

Reply to the above (first letter, distributorship)

SIMSON PUBLISHING HOUSE
Rockefeller Complex,
New York.

M/s. Hardford Book Co.,
Norton Road,
New Jersey.

21st Nov., 19____

Dear Sirs,

Re: **Distributorship**

We thank you for your letter dated 18th November, 19____, on the above subject.

We wish to inform you that we have no system of appointing any single distributor in any city. However, we can consider about your appointment as one of our wholesaler, for Calcutta on the following terms and conditions:—

1. That we shall allow you a discount of 25% + 10%.
2. That you will guarantee us a minimum monthly sale of US $5,000.
3. That all the goods will be supplied F.O.R. by rail. Where, however, the goods are required by transport, half expenses will have to be borne by you.
4. That all bills will be settled within 30 days.
5. That unsold books in saleable condition can be exchanged with our other publications.
6. That under no circumstances, you will allow more than 25% in the market.
7. That in case the annual turnover exceeds a net value of US $100,000, 2% extra discount will be allowed on the total bill value during one financial year.

In case you accept the above terms, please send us your order and confirmation.

Two copies of our latest catalogue are enclosed.

Yours faithfully,
For Simson Publishing House

Encl:— (1) Catalogue.

Counter Reply to the above

26th Nov., 19____

Messrs Simson Publishing House,
Rockefeller Complex,
New York.

We thank you for your letter dated 21st Nov. 19____.

The terms stated by you are acceptable to us and we have the pleasure of enclosing our first Order for US $8000.

Yours faithfully,
For Hardford Book Company
Sd/-

Reply to the Above (second letter, distributorship)

SIMSON PUBLISHING HOUSE
Rockefeller Complex,
New York.

20th May, 19____

Mr. Robert Nelson,
Managing Partner,
Book Traders,
California.

Dear Mr. Robert,

I write with reference to your letter of May 11, 19____ regarding your book THE LEGENDS by Mr. William Maxmueller.

Much as we would like to take up your publication for distribution, we regret our inability to do so, as at the present moment our hands are too full and we shall not be able to do justice to any new arrangement. Our thanks, however, for considering us as the possible distributor for your book.

Yours sincerely,
Alan Bevin
Managing Partner

Applying for an Agency

OVERSEAS RADIO CORPORATION
15 Crawford Street,
Dover.

18th Dec., 19____

Ref. No. RRC/93
Messrs Samson Radio & Television Industries,
Nelson Square,
London.

Dear Sirs,

This is in reply to your Advertisement in today's 'The Mirror' for appointing a single Distributor of your products in Dover.

We have pleasure in submitting the following details for your information:—

1. We have an excellent showroom measuring 71' x 56' (largest in the country) in the main shopping centre of the city.

2. Our annual net sales exceed £600000.

3. We can deposit a sum of £10000 as security.

4. We can guarantee a monthly sale of:—

200 Sets of Transistors

200 Sets of Radios

100 sets of large CTVs

50 sets of small CTVs

5. We shall pay all the bills within 45 days from the date of receipt of goods.

6. We would expect a minimum of 3% extra discount over and above thc 15% advertised by you.

7. The goods will be sent to us as per F.O.R.

8. The agency can be terminated by either party by giving 2 months' notice and in that case all unsold goods will be returned to you and our payments for the same together with our security of £10000 should be paid back within one month from the date of termination of the agency.

We hope you will find the above terms acceptable and will favour us with your reply per return of post.

Yours faithfully,
For Overseas Radio Corpn.
Sd/-
Manager

Reply to the Above

M/S. SAMSON RADIO & TELEVISION INDUSTRIES

Nelson Square,
London.

26th Dec., 19____

Messrs Overseas Radio Corporation,
15 Crawford Street,
Dover.

Dear Sirs,

We thank you for your letter dated 18th Dec. 19____ bearing No. RRC/93 and have pleasure in informing you that we agree to accept all your terms except that the payments will be made within 30 days from the date of issue of the bills.

On receipt of your confirmation, we shall forward to you our Agreement Form.

Thank you.

Yours faithfully,
For Samson Radio & Television Industries.
Sd/-

Counter Reply

OVERSEAS RADIO CORPORATION
15 Crawford Street, Dover.

29th Dec.,19____

Messers Samson Radio & Television Industries,
Nelson Square,
London.

Dear Sirs,

We thank you for your letter dated 26th December 19____, and agree to your proposal of making payments within 30 days.

While you send us the agency form for our signatures, we are enclosing our cheque for £10000 towards security amount together with our initial order.

Assuring you of our best co-operation.

Yours faithfully,
For Overseas Radio Corporation
Sd/-
Manager

13
Enquiries, Quotations and their Replies

Asking for Catalogue

HUDSON BOOKS
Ocean View Plaza,
Florida.

16th Oct., 19____

M/s. Simson Publishing House,
Rockefeller Complex,
New York.

Dear Sirs,

Please send us a copy of your latest catalogue together with best wholesale trade terms.

Yours faithfully,
For Hudson Books.
Sd/-

Reply to the Above

Messrs Hudson Books,
Ocean View Plaza,
Florida.

Dear Sirs,

We thank you for your letter dated 16th October, 19____ and have pleasure in enclosing a copy of our catalogue.

Our usual trade discount is 25%. However, in addition to this 10% discount is allowed to the wholesalers provided the minimum order is for US $5000.

All the goods are sent per F.O.R. by rail while in case of the goods through road transport and post, half the expenses are added in the bill.

The documents are sent through bank only.

As our books are widely advertised and circulated throughout USA, our clients are harvesting heavy profits in keeping bulk stock of our publications.

We shall be glad to hear further in the matter.

Thanking you,

Yours faithfully,
For Simson Publishing House
Sd/-

Calling Quotations for Electrical Bulbs and Tubes

REGAL DEPARTMENTAL STORE
Old County Road,
Bristol.

13th Jan., 19____

Messrs Lords Electricals,
Golf Road, Bristol.

Dear Sirs,

Please send us for lowest quotations for the following :-

1. 20 Bulb 100 W.
2. 20 Bulbs 60 W.
3. 40 Tubes (full size)
4. 60 Tubes (half size)

Thank you.

Yours faithfully,
For Regal Departmental Store
Sd/-

Reply to the Above

LORDS ELECTRICALS
Golf Road,
Bristol.

15th Jan., 19____

Messrs Regal Departmental Store,
Old County Road, Bristol.

Dear Sirs,

We thank you for your inquiry of 13th Jan. 19____ and have pleasure in quoting as under:—

1. 20 Bulbs 100 W. £ 1.00 each
2. 20 Bulbs 60 W. £ 0.80 each
3. 40 Tubes (full size) £ 20.00 each
4. 60 Tubes (half size) £ 11.60 each

Installation charges for each bulb are £0.50 and for each tube £1.00.

Thank you.

Yours faithfully,
For Lords Electricals,
Sd/-

Enquiry for Steel Furniture

NATIONAL PRODUCTIVITY COUNCIL

London

March, 13, 19____

Ref. No. 103

Messrs Johnson Steel Industries,
Glasgow.

Dear Sirs,

Please send us your lowest quotations for—

1. Storewell Cupboard measuring 78" x 36" x 19" with six adjustable shelves. 10
2. Three-Drawer fullscape size filing cabinets measuring 29½" high x 8½" wide x 27½" deep fitted with automatic lock, ball bearing slides and compressor plates. 15
3. Steel Trays 50
4. Steel Chairs (staff) 100

5. Steel Chairs (officers) 15

Quotations should reach us by 23rd March, 19____

Yours faithfully,
Secretary
National Productivity Council.

Reply to the Above

JOHNSON STEEL INDUSTRIES
Glasgow

21st March 19____

DS/11/103
The Secretary,
National Productivity Council,
London.

Dear Sirs,

We thank you for your inquiry No. 103 dated 13th March, 19____ and have pleasure in submitting our estimates as under:—

1. 10 Storewell Cupboards measuring 78" x 36" x 19" with six adjustable shelves. £100
2. 15 Filing Cabinets, fullscape size Code NF. each measuring 29½" x 8½" x 27½" having three drawers, running smoothly on ball-bearing suspensions, each drawer with compressor, label-holder and handle, complete with automatic locking device £110 each
3. 50 Steel Trays £3 each
4. 100 Steel Chairs for staff £12 each
5. 15 Steel Chairs for officers £20 each

Prices — All prices are inclusive of free delivery at your premises.

Colour — Olive Green.

Goods Tax — Will be charged extra at 10%.

Delivery — 15 days.

Payment — Full payment to be made within 15 days from the date of receipt of the goods.

Validity—The offer is valid for 60 days from date.

Our detailed leaflets on the above items are enclosed for your further information.

All parts of the material will be subject to a thorough anti-rust chemical and mechanical treatment before being applied a coat of anti-corrosive paint and sprayed under pressure with finest oven-baked enamel.

As we have got a stockist in London, we are forwarding your enquiry and our reply to him. All further correspondence on the subject may please be made with.

Messrs. Becker Steel Furniture,
17 Watson Street,
London.

Thank you.

Yours faithfully,
For Johnson Steel Industries.
Sd/-
Sales Manager.

Copy of M/s. Becker Steel furniture, 17 Watson Street, London.

Acknowledging Request for Quotation

19th Nov., 19____

Dear Sirs,

We are very much obliged for your letter of 2nd Nov. 19____ asking us to quote for ____________. Since the item is not easily available in the market and as we wish to offer it to you at the lowest possible price, we are making special enquiries for the same and will write to you in about a fortnight's time.

In the meanwhile we thank you once again and assure you of our best co-operation, always.

Yours faithfully,
For Crompton Agencies,
Sd/-

Enquiry for Hosiery

SUNBEAM TRADERS
Halls Steet,
Sydney.

15th April, 19____

Messrs. Easy Stocks (Pvt.) Ltd.,
Adelaide.

Dear Sirs,

Please send us your quotations for the following:—

1. 20 Doz. Nylon Socks (Free Size) Code N5
2. 30 Doz. Underwears (Full Size) Code U2
3. 50 Doz. Handkerchiefs (Gents) Code HI
4. 50 Doz. Handkerchiefs (Ladies) Code H3

The above are required as part of an order received from Singapore and will have to compete in quality and price with the Chinese and Japanese goods which are freely available there.

While quoting for the different qualities, please ensure that you will be in a position to execute the repeat bulk orders for exactly the same quality.

The goods will have to be packed in wooden cases and sent F.O.R. Sydney.

Yours faithfully,
For Sunbeam Traders
Sd/-

Reply to Above

23rd April, 19____

Messrs Sunbeam Traders,
Sydney.

Dear Sirs,

In reply to your inquiry of 15th April, 19____ we are pleased to quote as under:

1. 20 Doz. Nylon Socks (Free Size — all colours except Dark Orange) US $10 per doz.
2. 30 Doz. Underwears (Full size — white, creamish and light blue) US $10 per doz.
3. 50 Doz. Handkerchief (Gents — all colour — plain and printed) US $5 per doz.
4. 50 Doz. Handkerchief (Ladies — all colours — plain and printed) US $5 per doz.

less 12½ per cent usual discount plus 2½ per cent special discount for export.

Under separate registered post, we have today sent one sample each of the four items.

You will observe from the samples that the quality of our products and their prices can compete with any foreign market as we are ourselves exporting goods to the tune of US $2 million every year.

Our products are made in new Stylish finish and we can guarantee them to be unshrinkable. Further, they preserve the softness and elasticity and permit free passage of the perspiration which is very essential for health reasons.

In view of the above advantages, we are confident that our products will meet your fullest requirements and you will favour us with your bulk orders, always.

Yours faithfully,
For Easy Stocks (Pvt.) Ltd.
Sd/-

Enquiring about the Pocket Transistors

23, North Hill Road,
Melbourne.
15th Dec. 19____

Messrs Pocket Transistor Corporation,
17, South End Street,
Perth.

Dear Sirs,

I am interested in buying two sets of pocket transistors, advertised by you in the Illustrated Weekly of India of 24th November, 19____.

Please let me know the name of your local dealer in Patiala from whom I may buy the sets.

Yours faithfully,
Sd/-
Rex Harrison

Reply to the Above

18th December, 19____

Mr. Rex Harrison,
23, North Hill Road,
Melbourne.

Dear Sir,

We thank you for your letter dated 15th December, 19____.

You may buy the pocket Transistors from:—

M/s. Hoyale Bros. & Sons
Radio Dealers,
Near Railway Station,
Melbourne.

Thanking you,

Yours faithfully,
For Pocket Transistor Corporation,
Sd/-

Another Reply to Above

18th December 19.......

Mr. Rex Harrison,
23, North Hill Road,
Melbourne.

Dear Sirs,

We thank you for your letter dated 15th December, 19____.

We have not yet appointed any stockist in Melbourne and as such we would suggest you to procure the pocket transistors through VPP from us, direct.

Thanking you,

Yours faithfully,
For Pocket Transistor Corpn.
Sd/-

Reminder for Quotations

KARTAR TIMBER INDUSTRIES
Kathmandu,
(Nepal).

16th August, 19____

M/s New Light Publishers,
B-8, Sea View, Penany,
Singapore.

Sub:— Our Enquiry No. PC/445/6—dated 6-7-19— for the supply for Timber Calculator — 20 copies.

Dear Sirs,

Please refer to our enquiry under reference.

In this connection, we wish to state that we have not so far received your quotation against our subject enquiry. However, as a very special case, we are extending the due date for the receipt of the quotation against our subject enquiry up to 28-8-19____. If you are interested, please forward your quotation immediately, so as to reach here before the due date.

Your immediate compliance in this regard is requested.

Thanking you.

Yours faithfully,
For Kartar Timber Industries
Sd/-
Partner

Reply to the Above

Dated 22-8-19____

M/s. Kartar Timber Industries,
Kathmandu, Nepal.

Dear Sirs,

We thank you for your letter dated the 16th instant.

Please note that we have not received your letter dated 6-7-19____. We would appreciate if you could let us have a copy of the same to enable us to take further action in the matter.

Thank you.

Yours faithfully,
For New Light Publishers,
Sd/-

To Enlist Name for Enquiries regarding Machines

Ontario, Phone: 235212

MIDDLETON BROTHERS, Pvt. Ltd.

Manufacturers, Representatives Printers & Suppliers,
17 Central Avenue,
Ontario.

Dated 10-9-19—

Messrs Megregor Publishers,
Ontario.

Dear Sirs,

We shall be thankful if you kindly enlist our name on your mailing list for the enquiries in connection with the machines, equipments and materials including printing types required for Printing and Book Binding industry.

We trust we shall be able to serve you better by making supply of quality goods at moderate prices.

We confidently hope that you will kindly send us your esteemed enquiries whenever you happen to visit the market.

For your ready reference, we are sending herewith a few of our current price-lists and we trust you will find some of the offered items suitable for your immediate requirements.

We may add here that we are registered with all the Central, State, Semi and Quasi Government Presses as well as almost all the universities.

We are always at your service,

Thank you.

Yours faithfully,
For Middleton Bros. Pvt. Ltd.
Sd/-

Encl: As stated.

Enclosure to Above

MIDDLETON BROTHERS PVT. LTD.

Manufacturers Representatives Printers & Suppliers
17, Central Avenue,
Ontario.

Dear Sirs,

We have pleasure to inform you that we can supply you the following Steel Composing Room Equipments:

1. Galley rack of 2, 3 and 4 tiers to hold 50, 75 and 100 galleys of any sizes;
2. Galley rack with door and locking arrangements to hold 100 galleys of any sizes;
3. Galley rack with locking bar;
4. Newspaper galley rack with random top;
5. 'L' shape Forme rack to hold 18, 24 and 36 formes;
6. Lead rule and Reglet rack;
7. Furniture and Reglet rack;
8. Type case-rack with or without random top;
9. Block storage cabinet;
10. Composing frame unit consisting of galley rack, case-rack, sorts-drawer, plate shelf, rack and double sided random top;
11. Compact make-up Desk;
12. Sorts storage rack with 180 sorts boxes;
13. Sorts storage cabinet with 99 sorts boxes, with door and locking arrangements.

Besides this, we can also supply steel galleys of double wall of any size as well as Compositors' Stools etc.

We will furnish our quotation with illustrated leaflets for your required items on receipt of your specific enquiry.

We may add for your information that we have already supplied the said items to various Government and Commercial presses where the same have been highly approved due to high quality and workmanship and also we are holding several orders for execution.

Thanking you and always at your service, we remain.

Yours faithfully,

For Middleton Brothers Pvt. Ltd.,

Sd/-

Informing a Customer Regarding Arrival of T.V. Sets

SUPER BAZAR
THE CO-OPERATIVE STORE LTD.,
Ottawa.

Dated: 18-6-19—

Mr. Timothi Smith
Justine Street,
Ottawa.

Sub: Supply of N.T. Television Set.

Dear Sir,

We have great pleasure in informing you that we are now in a position to supply you the N.T. Television set, booked by you with us, out of the limited stock we have so far received.

The price per set works out to be US $350 which is inclusive of cost, Duty. Voltage, Regulator, Goods tax, Antenna and Installation. Out of this, a sum of US $50 is already deposited by you towards antenna and installation charges. The balance amount of US $300 may kindly be deposited at our Connaught Road branch (T.V./Radio Counter, 4th floor) by 3rd June positively. Since the supply position is as yet very limited, kindly ensure that the amount asked for is deposited by you by the date indicated above, failing which we would be at liberty to offer the set to the next customer on our list.

Thank you.

Yours faithfully,
Sd/-
Radio & T.V. Department

14

Orders and their Execution

Requesting to send Goods care of GPO

148305
Col. G. Sandurs
C/o GPO Rome
Italy.
14th March, 19____

Messrs Swiss Watch Co.,
16 West-End Cinema,
Geneva.

Dear Sirs,

With reference to your Advertisement in the last month's Reader's Digest, please send me one 'Lady's Watch', costing US $150 through V.P.P.

Yours faithfully,
Sd/-
George Sandurs

Reply to the Above

SWISS WATCH COMPANY
16 West End Cinema,
Geneva.

19th March, 19—

Ref. No. SWC/-
Ms. George Sandurs,
C/o GPO Rome,
Italy.

Dear Sir,

With reference to your letter dated 14th March, 19—, we wish to inform you that since post office does not accept any VPPs, it is necessary that the amount may please be remitted in advance. Please, therefore, remit a sum of US $160 in advance by money order or a bank-draft as per details mentioned below:—

Cost of Lady's Watch Model A 113	US $ 150.00
Packing and Postage	10.00
Total	160.00

Thank you.

Yours Faithfully,
For Swiss Watch Co.,
Sd/-

Placing an Order for Books

HUDSON BOOKS
Ocean View Plaza,
Florida.

27th Oct., 19—

M/s. Simson Publishing House,
Rockefeller Complex,
New York.

Dear Sirs,

We thank you for your letter dated 21st Oct., 19— together with a catalogue of your publications.

We have pleasure in placing the following order:—

25 Selected Letters

25 Business Letters

25 Encyclopedia of General Knowledge

50 Current Affairs

50 3000 Quotations

15 Office Procedure and Drafting

15 Good Thoughts

15 Timber Calculator

15 Top Ready Reckoner

10 Paradise Lost

10 Arons and The Man

10 The Roman Empire

10 War of Roses

5 Martin Luther King

Please send the goods by passenger train F.O.R. Manipur and forward the documents through the Florida American Express.

Thank you.

Yours faithfully,
For Hudson Books,
Sd/-

Reply to the Above

2nd Nov., 19—

M/s. Hudson Books,
Ocean View Plaza,
Florida.

Dear Sirs,

In compliance with your Order dated 27th October, 19____, we have pleasure in informing you that we have sent the parcel of goods by passenger train and forwarded the documents through your bankers.

A copy of the invoice is enclosed for your prior information.

Please release the documents on presentation.

Thanking you and assuring you of our best co-operation always.

Yours faithfully,
For Simson Publishing House
Sd/-

Encl:— Copy of Invoice.

Placing Order for Electric Bulbs and Tubes

REGAL DEPARTMENTAL STORE
Old County Road,
Bristol.

22nd Jan., 19—

Messrs Lord's Electricals,
Bristol.

Dear Sirs,

With further reference to your letter dated 15th Jan., 19— and our telephonic talk of this morning, we confirm our order as under:—

1. 18 Bulbs 10 W. @ US $2.00 each
2. 22 Bulbs 60 W. @ US $1.50 each
3. 30 Tubes (full size) @ US $20.00 each
4. 70 Tubes (small size) @ US $18.00 each
5. Installation charges US $25.00 for the whole job.

Please send your electrician immediately on receipt of this letter as the Departmental Store will start functioning from the 16th February, 19____.

Yours faithfully,

For Regal Departmental Store,

Sd/-

Reply to the Above

There is no need for any written reply from M/s. Lord's Electricals as the subject had been discussed on telephone. The bill can be sent through the electrician.

Placing an Order for Steel Furniture

NATIONAL PRODUCTIVITY COUNCIL

London.

March 29, 19____

Messrs Becker Steel Furniture,
17, Watson Road,
London.

Dear Sirs,

With further reference to the personal visit of your representative to our office, last evening, we are pleased to place our following order with you:—

1. 6 Storewell Cupboards 78" x 6" x 19" 6 shelves — US $100 each.
2. 153-Drawer fool scap size filing cabinets 29½" x 8½" x 27½" — US $110 each.
3. 50 Steel Trays — US $3 each.
4. 80 Staff Chairs — US $12 each.
5. 15 Officer Chairs — US $25 each.

Please send your bill in duplicate.

Thank you.

Yours faithfully,
Sd/-
Secretary
National Productivity Council

Reply to the Above

3rd April, 19____

The Secretary,
National Productivity Council,
London.

Dear Sir,

We thank you for your order dated 29th March, 19____.

We are sending the goods through our transport and forwarding agents herewith our bill in duplicate. Please arrange an early payment of the same.

Thanking you once again and assuring you of our best co-operation always.

Yours faithfully,
For M/s. Becker Steel Furniture
Sd/-

Encl: Bill in Duplicate

Order for Hosiery

SUNBEAM TRADERS
15, Halls Street,
Sydney.

1st May, 19____

Easy Stocks,
Adelaide.

Dear Sirs,

We thank you for your letter dated 23rd April, 19____ The registered packet of samples has also been received.

We shall appreciate by our despatching all the goods except 30 Doz. Underwears as the price quoted by you is a bit high. However, in case you can reduce the price to US $9.00 per doz. this item may also be included.

Please forward the documents through Citi Bank, M.G. Road, Sydney.

Thank you.

Yours faithfully,
For Sunbeam Traders,
Sd/-

Reply to the Above

11th May, 19____

EASY STOCKS
Adelaide.

M/s. Sunbeam Traders,
Halls Street,
Sydney.

Dear Sirs,

We thank you for your order dated the 1st May, 19____. We have this day sent the goods per passenger train and forwarded the document through the Citi Bank, M.G. Road, Sydney.

We have not been able to include 30 Doz. of underwears as the price of US $10.00 quoted by us is the barest minimum we can afford.

A copy of the bill is enclosed.

Thank you.

Yours faithfully,
For Easy Stocks
Sd/-

Order for Pocket Transistors

23, North Hill Road,
Melbourne.
24th Dec., 19—

Messrs Pocket Transistors Corporation,
17, South End Street,
Perth.

Dear Sirs,

With reference to your letter dated 18th December, 19—, please send me two sets of pocket transistors through VPP, at the above address.

The VPP will be honored on presentation.

Thank you.

Yours faithfully,
Sd/-
Rex Harrison

Reply to the above

POCKET TRANSISTORS CORPORATION
17, South End Street,
Perth.

Date 29-12-19—

Dear Friend,

In compliance with your order dated 24-12-19—, we have pleasure in informing you that we have today sent the following goods through V.P.P. which please honour on presentation.

Particulars	Amount
	US $
2 Pocket Transistors	20.00
Goods Tax	2.00
	22.00
Add Packing & Postage	5.00
Net	27.00

Yours faithfully,
For Pocket Transistors Corpn.
Sl./Manager

Ordering Goods at Old Prices

Duckle Buck Finn,
Meadow Road,
Liverpool.
11th February, 19—

Messrs Walcott Pencil Industries,
Old Church Road,
New Hampshire.

Dear Sirs,

Please send me 10 Gross HB 2 pencils at £20.00 per gross through V.P.P.

Thank you.

Yours faithfully,
Sd/-
D.B. Finn

Reply to the Above

Mr. D.B. Finn,
Meadow Road,
Liverpool.

17th Feb., 19—

Dear Sir,

We thank you very much for your letter dated 11th February, 19— placing with us an order for 10 gross HB 2 pencils.

It appears that you have with you our old catalogue. The prices have been revised from 1st Jan., this year and current price of HB 2 pencils is £2.50 per gross.

We shall, therefore, appreciate your sending us a fresh order which will receive our immediate attention.

In the meanwhile we thank you and await your valued order.

Yours faithfully,
For Walcott Pencil Industries.
Sd/-

Counter Reply

Mr. D.B. Finn may send a letter for ordering goods in case the price of £1.50 per gross is acceptable to him. In other case normally no reply is sent.

15
Cancellations and Complaints Regarding Orders

Telegram Cancelling an Order

ELITE	BOMBAY	
REFER	LETTER	TENTH
CANCEL	ORDER	LETTER
FOLLOWS		

EMKAY TRADERS
BOSTON

Letter Referring to the Above Telegram

EMKAY TRADERS
Royal Palace,
USA.

12th Nov., 19____

Messrs Elite Auto Parts,
Opera House,
Boston.

Dear Sirs,

We confirm having sent the following telegram today.

REFER LETTER TENTH CANCEL
ORDER LETTER FOLLOWS

We very much regret to have cancelled our order dated 10th Nov., 19—, for supply of 10 boxes of MK 14 screws. This necessity has arisen as our store-keeper did not make an entry for receipt of 120 boxes last month and thus our stock register did not show the correct position at the time of placing the order. We may, therefore, not require any supplies for another three months. On the other hand, we assure you that we shall place a bulk order with you as soon as the occasion arises.

In case you incur any loss on this account, please debit the amount to our account and include the same in our next bill.

Thank you.

Yours faithfully,
For Emkay Traders,
Sd/-

Reply to the Above

ELITE AUTO PARTS
Boston

12th Nov., 19____

Messrs Emkay Traders,
Royal Palace,
USA.

Dear Sirs,

We were about to send the goods of your order through our forwarding agent, when we received your telegram. Your letter of 12th November, 19— has also been received.

As advised by you, we have withheld the despatch of the goods. We have incurred an expenditure of US $30 towards packing of the goods and we do hope that you would not mind, if we debit the same to your account.

In the meanwhile, we thank you once again and assure you of our best co-operation always.

Yours faithfully,
For Elite Auto Parts,
Sd/-

Counter Reply

EMKAY TRADERS
Royal Palace
USA.

18th Nov., 19____

Messrs Elite Auto Parts,
Opera House,
Boston.

Dear Sirs,

We thank you for your letter dated 15th November, 19____.

We are enclosing the Drafts No. ______ dated ____ for US $30 towards the packing-expenses incurred by you.

Thank you.

Yours faithfully,
For Emkay Traders,
Sd/-

Alternatively substitute the sentence: Please debit the amount of US $30 to our account and include the same in our next bill.

Informing the Client Regarding Despatch of Goods before Receipt of Telegram

ELITE AUTO PARTS
New Jersey Road,
USA.

15 Nov. 19____

Messrs Emkay Traders,
Clinton Road, USA.

Dear Sirs,

We are in receipt of your telegram and letter of 12th Nov., 19____.

Your order dated 10th November reached us by the first mail of 11th Nov. As this was marked urgent, we immediately got the goods packed and handed over the same to our forwarding agent, whole in turn got them loaded in their presence, the same evening.

On receipt of your telegram, we telephoned the transport company and were informed that the consignment had already left their premises.

As the things are beyond our reach at this stage, we shall very much appreciate your arranging to take delivery of the goods.

However, for your convenience, we are advising your banker to deliver the documents to you against 30 days sight instead of cash payment.

Thanking you once again and assuring you of our best co-operation, always.

Yours faithfully,
For Elite Auto Parts,
Sd/-

Informing Suppliers Regarding Non-Arrival of Goods

CHRISTIAN SOCIETY

Park County,

London.

Messrs Tucker & Sons,

Canal Road,

Leeds.

Ref: Your Invoice No 1762 dated 10-3-19—

Dear Sirs,

With reference to the above invoice we are sorry to inform you that we have not received the goods so far. The bill is already paid.

Please look into the matter and let us have your reply per return of post.

Yours faithfully,

Sd/-

Dan Joseph

Manager

Sales Department

Reply to the above

TUCKER & SONS

Canal Road,

Leads.

16th May, 19____

M/s. Christian Society,

Park County,

London.

Dear Sirs,

We thank you for your letter dated 13th May, 19____ and regret very much to note that you have not yet received the consignment of your Invoice No. 1762.

We have today checked up the matter with the railway authorities here and have been informed that they loaded the goods in 13Dn on 11th March, 19____ They, however, suggest that you may approach the Station

Superintendent of your town and ask him to send a telegram to locate the parcel.

Thank you.

Yours faithfully,
For Tucker & Sons,
Sd/-

Complaint for Shortage of Goods

HALLIS AND RANSON
17 Welsh Street,
London.

11th Feb., 19____

M/s. Dexter & Sons,
Old Square,
Birmingham.

Dear Sirs,

We have taken delivery of the consignment sent against PWB No. 123468 dated 19th January, 19____.

On opening the parcel, we have observed that 12 copies of 'Jokes For All' are not there. We shall, therefore, appreciate your sending us the same through registered post. Alternatively please issue us the necessary credit note.

Thank you.

Yours faithfully,
For Hallis and Ranson
Sd/-

Reply to the above

DEXTER & SONS
Old Square,
Birmingham.

14th Feb., 19____

Messrs Hallis and Ranson,
17 Welsh Street,
London.

Dear Sirs,

We thank you for your letter dated 11th February, 19____.

We are surprised to learn that you have observed a shortage of 12 copies of 'Jokes For All'. All our consignment are checked twice before packing and chances of any shortage, whatsoever, are minimised. As the items are checked individually and collectively, we wonder if you have received any other item in excess by the same number. We suggest that you may please have one more check of the consignment and in case you still feel the shortage as mentioned above, we shall be only too glad to compensate you for the same.

Thank you.

Yours faithfully,
For Dexter & Sons,
Sd/-

Another Reply

DEXTER & SONS
Old Square,
Birmingham.

14th Feb., 19____

Messrs Hallis & Ranson,
17, Welsh Street,
London.

Dear Sirs,

We thank you for your letter dated 11th Feb., 19____.

We regret that through an oversight, 12 copies of 'Jokes For All' were not included in the parcel. We are not arranging to send the same through registered post.

Assuring you to our best co-operation always.

Yours faithfully,
For Dexter & Sons,
Sd/-

Complaint Regarding Non-Execution of an Order

ALEX SMITH & SONS
New Complex,
Bristol.

11th Nov., 19____

Messrs Robertson & Co.,
Picadilly Circus,
London.

Dear Sirs,

With further reference to our order No. 103 dated 27th Sept., 19____ placed through your representative, Shri Manohar Lal, we regret very much to say that we have neither received the goods nor have we heard anything in the matter.

As the goods are urgently required, please despatch the same immediately, if not already done.

Thank you.

Yours faithfully,
For Alex Smith & Sons
Sd/-

Reply to the Above

ROBERTSON & CO.
Picadilly Circus,
London.

13th Nov., 19____

Messrs Alex Smith & Sons,
New Complex,
Bristol.

Dear Sirs,

We thank you for your letter dated 11th Nov., 19____.

As item Nos. 2 and 3 of your order were not ready with us and since these two items formed 75% of the total value of your order, we could not execute the order earlier. However, the goods have now been despatched on 10th November and we hope you would have received a copy of our invoice which was sent under separate post on the same date.

Thank you.

Yours faithfully,
For Robertson & Co.,
Sd/-

Complaint Regarding Receipt of Wrong Goods

RASHID MOHAMMED & SONS
Central Market,
Singapore.

18th August, 19____

M/s. Sultan Ahmed & Co.,
Razak Road,
Kuala Lumpur.

Dear Sirs,

We have today taken delivery of the consignment against PWB 173132 dated 19th July, 19____.

On opening the parcel, we were surprised to find that the contents of the same were entirely different from those ordered by us as per our letter No. A/171 dated 15th July, 19____.

Details of the Goods received are:

100 Packets White Paper 11 x 13

50 Packets Carbon (Jores)

125 Gross Blue Pencils

125 Gross Black Pencils

100 Gross Sanden Rubbers

200 Small Bottle Elephant Gum.

Please look into the matter immediately and let us have your reply per return of post.

Thank you.

Yours faithfully,
For Rashid Mohammed & Sons.,
Sd/-

Reply to the Above

SULTAN AHMED & CO.
Razak Road,
Kuala Lumpur.

3rd August, 19____

M/s Rashid Mohammed & Sons,
Central Market,
Singapore.

Dear Sirs,

We thank you for your letter dated 18th August, 19____ and are sorry to learn that through a mistake on the part of the railways you have received a wrong consignment.

The consignment received by you is meant for M/s. Book Traders who in turn have collected your parcel from the railways as we have received a letter from them also.

We have today written a letter to Messrs Book Traders requesting them to exchange their parcel with yours and a copy of the letter is enclosed.

We very much regret for the inconvenience caused.

Thank you.

Yours faithfully,
For Sultan Ahmed & Co.,
Sd/-

Encl: As above

Complaint Regarding Damaged Goods

POPULAR TEA DEPOT.
Malaysia.

16th Oct., 19____

M/s. Supreme Tea Industries,
Jakartha.

Dear Sirs,

We regret very much to say that your consignment against PWB No. 163821 dated 10th Sept., 19____, has been received in an entirely damaged condition and not a single packet is in saleable condition. Will you, therefore, please send a fresh consignment, on receipt of which we shall return the goods already received?

Thanking you.

Yours faithfully,
For Popular Tea Depot,
Sd/-

Reply to the above

SUPREME TEA INDUSTRIES
Jakartha.

19th Oct., 19____

Popular Tea Depot,
Malaysia.

Dear Sirs,

We thank you for your letter dated 16th October, 19____. We are sorry to learn that through a little negligence on the part of our packing department, you have received the consignment in a damaged condition.

While we are arranging to send a fresh consignment of your order within a day or two, we would suggest that you may sell the tea (already received) in the loose form and remit us the amount in due course at the rate of US $20 per 1b. instead of US $22 per 1b.

We regret once again for the inconvenience caused and assure you that such a thing will not happen in future as we have instructed our packing department to provide wooden packings hereafter.

Thank you.

Yours faithfully,
For Supreme Tea Industries,
Sd/-

16

Clearing and Forwarding Letters

Asking the Clearing Agents to contact regarding Business

BEAUTY SOAP INDUSTRIES
Singapore.

17th Oct., 19____

M/s. Ocean Clearing & Forwarding Co.,
Singapore.

Dear Sirs,

As you may be aware, we have a large number of in and out parcels daily and we would very much like to pass on the whole work of clearing and forwarding to you. However, before we decide in doing so, we shall appreciate your sending one of your representatives to our office to discuss business terms.

Thank you.

Yours faithfully,
For Beauty Soap Industries.
Sd/-

Reply to the Above

A line in reply seeking appointment may be written. Alternatively the appointment may be arranged even on telephone.

Sending R/R for Clearing Goods

BEAUTY SOAP INDUSTRIES
Singapore.

28th Oct., 19____

M/s. Ocean Clearing & Forwarding Co.,
Singapore.

Dear Sirs,

With further reference to the personal visit of your manager, Mr. Abdul Hamid, we have pleasure in enclosing 37 R/R duly endorsed in your favour.

Please take delivery of the parcels from the Railway Office and deliver the same to us.

Please send your bill in duplicate @ US $0.50 per R/R and the payment will be sent to you within ten days, as mutually agreed.

Thank you.

Yours faithfully,
For Beauty Soap Industries,
Sd/-

Manager

Reply to the Above

OCEAN CLEARING & FORWARDING COMPANY
Singapore.

29th Oct., 19____

M/s. Beauty Soap Industries,
Singapore.

Dear Sirs,

With reference to your letter dated 28th Oct., 19____, we are arranging to send 36 parcels through our Clearing agent. One parcel has not yet arrived and we have retained the R/R with us.

Our bill in duplicate is also enclosed.

Assuring you of our best co-operation always.

Yours faithfully,
For Ocean Clearing & Forwarding Co.,
Sd/-

Encl: Bill in Duplicate.

Asking the Clearing Agent to Collect Goods

BEAUTY SOAP INDUSTRIES
Singapore.

M/s. Ocean Clearing & Forwarding Co.,
Singapore.

Dear Sirs,

With further reference to our telephonic talk of yesterday, we wish to inform you that 120 Boxes—Full Truck load—are now ready and you may arrange to collect the same.

The goods may be sent to Singapore for onward shipment to Colombo through "S.S. Sri Lanka" leaving on 1st December.

Yours faithfully,
For Beauty Soap Industries,
Sd/-

Note:— Other letters regarding re-booking of goods, loss of R/Rs. Claims etc. are dealt with under Chapter 17 "Correspondence with the Railways and Road Transport Companies."

17
Correspondence with the Railways and Road Transport Companies

Despatch of goods by rail is done by filling up the particulars on the Forwarding Notes supplied by the Railways. Some private companies also have their own forwarding-notes printed, where the despatch of parcels is in a very large number.

Despatch by Road Transport is generally done on the basis of short description of goods given on the letter-head of consignor. However, some big transport companies insist for full details on their own forms (much similar to those of the Railways). A copy of invoice (in some cases two/ three) is almost essential with every forwarding note of the Road Transport Co.

Asking the Railway Authorities to Cancel PWB

SUPER CO.
Janab-el-Road,
Dubai.

4th April, 19____

The Chief Parcel Clerk,
UAE Rly, UAE.

Sub: PWB 178312. dt. 4th April, 19____

Dear Sir,

Immediately after handing over the parcel of goods to you against the above PWB, we have received a telegram from our clients advising us not to send the goods. We, therefore, request you to please cancel the above PWB, which is sent through bearer in original. As the freight has already been paid, please return the amount after making deduction of your cancellation charges.

Thank you.

Yours faithfully,
For Super Co.,
Sd/-

Re-Booking of Goods

RAHIM SPARE PARTS
Sultan Road,
Abu Dhabi (UAE).

Dated : 16th June, 19.....

The Station Superintendent,
Dubai.

Sub: PWB No. 163821 date 18th Feb., 19____

Dear Sir,

We are enclosing the above PWB.

Despite our best efforts, the party (for whom the goods were meant) has not released the goods and we are left with no choice except to get the goods re-booked. Hence this letter.

We shall appreciate your taking an immediate action in the matter.

Thank you.

Yours faithfully,
For Rahim Spare Parts,
Sd/-

Partner

Reply to the Above

Whereas the goods are lying at the destination station, the Station Supdt. will re-book the consignment and send the PWB under registered post to the consignor.

Sale Notice from Railways

Registered A.D.

From: Station Supdt. (Parcel).
Dubai.

To: Super Co.,
Janab-el-road,
Dubai.

24-1-19—

No. S 143/74

Sub: to Abu Dhabi
PWB 74348 Dated 10-11-19____
Sender: Super Co.,
Consignee: Self

Dear Sirs,

The above consignment of which you are the sender/consignee was received at the destination on 13-11-19____ and since then it is lying undelivered entirely at your risk and wharfage is accuring thereon every day.

As the consignment cannot be kept on hand indefinitely, I hereby serve you with this notice that if delivery is not effected within 15 days from the date of receipt of this letter, after paying the charges detailed below which are correctly due to the Railways up-to-date, the consignment will be treated as unclaimed property and sold by public auction under section 55 and 56 of the Indian Railways Act.

Details of charges	*Amount*
1. Freight charges	US $3.00
2. Under charge	—
3. Wharfage/Demurrage up-to-date (24-1-19____)	US $16.00
4. Other charges	US $1.70
	20.70

In the event of sale if the amount due to the Railways as detailed above is not covered by sale proceeds, you will be liable to pay the deficit amount.

Please send Instructions for Disposal direct to SM Sirsa under advice to this office.

Yours faithfully,
Signature: Sd/-
Designation: Station Supdt.
Dubai

Note:— While replying quote reference No. shown above.

Copy to: SM, Dubai, for information.

Signature: Sd/-
Designation: Station Supdt.
Dubai

Reply to the Above

Registered
SUPER CO.
Janab-el-Road
Duabi.

27th, 19____

The Station Supdt. (Parcel),
Abu Dhabi.

Sub: PWB No. 74338 dated 10-11-19____ ABUDHABI.

Dear Sir,

With reference to the Station Supdt., Abu Dhabi, letter No. 5143/74 dated 24th Jan. 19____, on the subject cited above, we request you to please retain the above parcel for a period of one month, as we are arranging to take delivery of the same.

Yours faithfully,
For Super Co.,
Sd/-
Partner

Copy to: Station Master.,

Dubai.

Rly. Authorities informing about Transfer of Goods to the Lost Property Office

From:
Station Supdt.
Dubai.

To
M/s. Anjan Spare Parts,
Alim Palea,
Dubai.

Dated 24/6/19—

Ref: No.: PI/LPO/FGN/73

Sub: PWB No. 163821 dated 18.2.19____
Ex-NDLS....Dubai.....Rc-Booking.

Dear Sir,

With reference to your letter dated 16 June 19____ on the subject cited above, I wish to inform you that since you did not arrange to take delivery of the parcel even after a sale notice from me, the goods have now been sent to LPO, Abu Dhabi, vide this office letter No. PI/LPO/FGN/73, dated 19th June, 19____. You may, if so desire, correspond with LPO, Abu Dhabi, to know about the latest position of the parcel.

Yours faithfully,
Signature : Sd/-
Designation : Station Supdt.
Dubai Railway.

Reply to the Above

The Consignor may now send a letter to the Lost Property Office, Madras, and ask for re-booking of the parcel.

Requesting for Open Delivery of Goods

M.N. DANGLAS & SONS
Station Road,
Karachi.

14th Feb., 19____

The Chief Parcel Clerk,
Karachi.

Sub: PWB 184213 dt. 17-1-19____

Ex DLKA.... Karachi

Dear Sir,

Our representative, who visited you yesterday for taking delivery of the above consignment, informs us that the parcel is lying in a torn condition. We, therefore, request you to please give us Open Delivery of the same.

Yours faithfully,
For M.N. Danglas & Sons
Sd/-

N.B. The original invoice of goods is also sent herewith.

Shortage Certificate of Goods by Railways

PWB No. 184213 dt. 17-1-19____

Ex DLKA.... Karachi

Delivery of the above consignment made with the following remarks.

The parcel found in torn condition weighing 8 kgs against 10 kgs, and following goods found short as per invoice produced by the Party.

6 Nos. N 2 Screws @ 5/- each	30.00 US$
2 Nos. N 1 Screws @ 3/- each	6.00 US$
5 Nos. N 3 Screws @ 7/- each	35.00 US$
1 Nos. N 8 Screws @ 2/- each	2.00 US$
Total	73.00 US$

Sd/-
Station Supdt. (Parcels),
Karachi

Requesting Railway Authorities for Exemption of Wharfage etc.

TINY POCKET BOOKS
White Plains,
New York.

The Superintendent,
D.S. Office,
New York.

Sub: PWB No.: 703244 dated 20-8-19____
Ex: BDME to New York.

Dear Sirs,

We enclose PWB as per details mentioned above.

Despite our best efforts it has not been possible to take delivery of the consignment at its destination station and as such the consignment has incurred heavy wharfage. On the other hand the books of the consignment have now become outdated and most of them are not saleable.

Since we have suffered heavy loss in the consignment under reference, we shall feel much obliged if you very kindly grant us exemption from all the expenses except freight which we shall gladly pay.

Thank you.

Yours faithfully,
For Tiny Pocket Books
Sd/-

Loss of K/R PWB

HI-FI CO.
Morello Ave,
California.

29th March, 19____

The Chief Parcel Clerk,
California.
Dear Sir,

Sub: PDB No. 123456 dated 29-3-19____

NWLS to California

We are informed by our clients that they have lost the above PWB. We shall, therefore, very much appreciate your issuing us a Duplicate PWB.

Thank you.

Yours faithfully,
For HI-FI Co.,
Sd/-
Partner

Reply to the Above

From: The Chief Parcel Clerk,
California.

To: HI-FI Co.
Morello Ave, California.
13th April, 19____

No. - N/837

Sub: PWB No. 123456 of 20-3-19____

Dear Sirs,

With refcrence to your letter No. Nil dated 29th March, 19____, on the subject cited above, I have to inform you that there is no system of issuing a Duplicate PWB in the railways. On the other hand an Indemnity Note on a Bond of US $1.50 is to be filled by you which will then be verified by us to enable you to take delivery of the consignment.

A specimen of Indeminty Note is enclosed for your convenience.

Yours faithfully,
Signature Sd/-
Designation: Chief Parcel Clerk
California.

Encl: As above

*In case of a Self PWB the Indemnity Note is to be filled in by the sender at the Rly. station of despatch of goods while in case where the PWB is in the name of the Party, the Indeminty Note is to be filled up by him at destination.

Specimen of the Indemnity Note

INDEMNITY NOTE

I hereby acknowledge to have received from the Railway .... valued at US$ ...... which was despatched to my address from the ...... station of the ...... Railway on or about the ..... day of ..... the Railway receipt for which has been .... and for myself, my heir, executors and administrators I undertake on consideration of such a delivery as aforesaid to hold the President of India, his agent and servant/Railway Administration, its agents and servants harmless and indemnified in respect of all the claims to the said goods.

And I, the undersigned, signing below the consignee of these goods certify that the first signor is the bonafide owner of the goods, and that I undertake the whole of the said liability equally with the consignee and for this purpose I affix my signature hereto.

Signature of Witness	Signature of Consignee ....
Father's Name	Father's Name ....
Caste .... Age	Caste .... Age ....
Residence	Residence ....
Profession	Profession ....
Witness	Surety ....
Father's Name	Father's Name ....
Caste .... Age	Caste .... Age ....
Profession	Profession ....
Residence	Residence ....

Executed in my presence.

Station stamp   Station Master

*Before submitting the Indemnity Note to the Railway Authorities, signatures of the consignee must be got attested from his banker.

Requesting the Railway Authorities to Verify an Indemnity Note

HI-FI CO.

Morello Ave, California.

4th April, 19____

The Chief Parcel Clerk,
Canada

Sub : PWB No. 123456 of 20-3-19____

Dear Sir,

We are sending through bearer an Indemnity Note for the above PWB.

Please verify the same and return through the bearer.

Thank you.

Yours faithfully,
For HI-FI Co.,
Sd/-

Submitting a Claim for Goods

Registered A.D.

ALFA TRADERS
Karachi.

17th Nov., 19____

Chief Commercial Supdt.
Lahore,
Pakistan.

Sub: PWB No. 183878 dated 8th June, 19____

Karachi–Lahore.

Dear Sir,

We have been informed by the Chief Parcel Clerk of Karachi that the consignment against the above PWB has not reached the destination so far.

As 5 months* have already passed since we sent the goods, it appears that the parcel has been lost in transit. We are, therefore, enclosing the above PWB in original together with our invoice No. 183 dated 18-6-19____ for US $25.60 and shall appreciate your passing our claim at an early date.

Yours faithfully,

For Alfa Traders,
Sd/-

*All claims must be lodged within 6 months from the date of booking the goods, otherwise, the same will not be entertained.

Note : While submitting a claim, a letter of Authority for payment must be obtained from the consignee which should be verified by the Station Superintendent of Destination Railway Station.

Acknowledgment of Claim

CHIEF COMMERCIAL SUPDT.
Lahore, Pakistan.

3rd Dec., 19____

No. CDA-5-183878/18-6-19____
Lahore- Karachi,
M/s. Alfa Traders.
Karachi.

Dear Sirs,

I beg to acknowledge receipt of your letter dated 17th Nov., 19____.

Such action as may be considered necessary will be taken.

Yours faithfully,
For Chief Commercial Supdt.
Sd/-

Important Hints for the Information of the Claimants

To facilitate disposal of your claim the following should be complied with:—

Furnish details showing now the amount claimed has been arrived at and submit the sender's sale-invoice in original in support of the same and also the following:—

(*a*) Short Certificate, assessment memo, letter from the firm that paid freight and effected delivery authorizing you to receive payment must also be furnished.

(*b*) As far as possible, either the original or at least a true copy of the original Railway Receipt should be submitted with the letter of claim.

(*c*) In the case of missing luggage, a full description of the missing package (such as, a wooden box, steel trunk, suitcase hat-box or bundle, or without pad-locks, gunny covering, any label, address or distinguishing mark) should be furnished along with its size, shape, colour as well as details of contents of each individual package along with the respective values of each item contained therein.

Letter from the Railways regarding Payment of claim

PAKISTAN RAILWAY
Karachi

18th Feb., 19____

No. 5818 CH/MBg/105/71,
Messrs. Afga Traders,
Rawalpindi,
Pakistan.

Ex.:— Rawalpindi — Lahore

Inv/P.W. Bill 183878 R.R...... dt. 18-6-19—

Ref:— Your letter No........... dated ....

Dear Sirs,

I offer you US $70.80 (Dollar Seventy and Eighty only) in full and final settlement of your claim with the commitment that if the goods are subsequently received, you will take its delivery and refund the amount paid.

Please convey your acceptance within 10 days from the date of receipt of this letter failing which papers at this end will be filed.

This is without prejudice.

Yours faithfully,
For Chief Commercial Superintendent,
Sd/-

Reply to the Above

AFGA TRADERS
Rawalpindi.

24th Feb., 19____

Pakistan Railway.,
Karachi,
Pakistan.

Sub : PWB No. 183878

Ex Rawalpindi – Lahore

Dear Sirs,

With reference to your letter No. 5818 CII/MBG/105/71 dated the 18th Feb., 19____, on the subject cited above, this is to request you to please favour us with a Bank Draft of US $70.80 per return of post towards full settlement of the above claim.

Yours faithfully,
For Alfa Traders,
Sd/-

Asking Road Transport Company to Re-Book Parcel

Registered

PEOPLE'S STORES

Centre Road,
Kuala Lumpur.

M/s. Air Transport Company,
Beach Road,
Penang.

Sub:— G.R.17101 of 5-8-19—

Ex. Kuala Lumpur — Penang

Dear Sir,

We are enclosing the above G.R. with a request to please re-book the consignment to Kuala Lumpur.

Thank you.

Yours faithfully,
For People's Stores
Sd/-
Manager.

Reply to the Above

AIR TRANSPORT COMPANY

Beach Road,
Penang.

23rd Sept., 19____

M/s. People's Stores,
Central Road,
Kuala Lumpur.

Sub: G.R. 17101 - 5-8-19____ *Kuala Lumpur—Penang*

Dear Sir,

With reference to your letter dated 16th September, 19____, on the subject referred to above, please note that we cannot re-book the consignment unless we receive the re-booking advice from Kuala Lumpur office. Please, therefore, contact them at your earliest and get the needful done. In the meanwhile please send a copy of your invoice.

Thanking you.

Yours faithfully,
For Air Transport Co.,
Sd/-
Manager.

Copy to the Head Office, Delhi.

Asking the Head Office to send an Advice

PEOPLE'S STORES
Central Road,
Kuala Lumpur.

27th Sept., 19____

M/s. Air Transport Company,
Beach Road,
Penang.

Sub: 1710 dated 15-8-19____ - *Ex.* Kuala Lumpur
Penang Re-booking.

Dear Sir,

With further reference to your branch office letter dated 23rd September, on the subject referred to above (a copy forwarded to you also), we shall appreciate your sending immediate instructions to them for re-booking the consignment to Kuala Lumpur.

A copy of our invoice is enclosed herewith.

Thank you.

Yours faithfully,
For People's Stores,
Sd/-
Manager.

Head Office's Letter (Advice) to Branch Office for Re-booking

AIR TRANSPORT COMPANY

Penang

Ref. No. ASR/NST/HO/RBKG/73. 760 dated 2nd Oct, 19____

The Manager,
Penang.

Sub: Re-booking for the Goods for GR No. 17101 dated 5-8-19____ *Ex.* Kuala Lumpur to Penang and back to Kuala Lumpur.

Dear Sir,

As per the instructions received from the consignors on the above subject, you are hereby directed to re-book the goods in question to Kuala Lumpur as usual-charging all your dues in your fresh GR, which maybe sent to the undernoted consignors in a registered cover under advice to the Head Office.

The goods were entrusted to .... vide your Transhipment Chart No. .... dated ...... which is being enclosed. Please recall the goods from the Associates and as soon as received back, the same may be re-booked as directed above.

In case the consignment is not fit for re-booking, the condition may be intimated to the Head Officc for further instructions before re-booking.

In case of insured GR (s), it is important that the goods are insured again for the same value charging premium as per the original GR.

Managing Director.

Encl:

(1) Invoice copy/copies

(2) Crossing GR/GRs

c.c to :—

1. M/s. People's Stores, Central Road, Kuala Lumpur, with reference to their letter, No. nil dated 27-9-19____.

2. ....

Managing Director.

Specimen of an Indemnity Note to be filled in, in case of Loss of a GR.

To

Station .... the ....

Dear Sir,

Re :- GR NO. ...... Dt..........
Consignor ....
Ex...................... to ....
Contents ....

I.......................................

S/o..of (address..)
Proprietor/Partner/Director/Manager of M/s...................... do hereby declare that we are the actual consignment note. The Consignee Copy of the said consignment note has been lost/misplaced from our possession.

Therefore, we shall be highly obliged if you kindly deliver us the consignment. Needless to mention here that I and our above firm individually and/or jointly will remain liable for all losses, damages, disputes, etc. arising out of this event and these will be settled within three days of receipt of such intimation from you/your agents/consignors or their authorised agents and their decisions will be binding on us.

Yours faithfully,
Sd/-
(Rubber Stamp & Signature)

18

Correspondence with a Post Office

Applying for V.P. Journal

JERRY THOMAS & SONS
President Road,
Boston.

18th July, 19____

To,
The Post Master,
Boston City.

Dear Sir,

As our daily average VPP has now reached 40, we would request you to please issue us the Special V.P. Journal.

Thank you.

Yours faithfully,
For Jerry Thomas & Sons
Sd/-
(Jerry Carus)

Reply to the Above

From: Post Master
Boston City,

To: M/s Jerry Thomas & Sons
President Road,
Boston.

No.

Dated 1st, Aug. _______

***Sub** : Issue of a special V.P. Journal*

Dear Sir,

With reference to your letter dated 18th July, ____, it is to inform you that the sanction for issue of special VP Journal has been received and you may send your representative to collect the same.

Yours faithfully,
Sd/-
Post Master

Opening a Saving Account

The Post Master,
Residency Road,
California.

Dear Sir,

As I wish to open a savings account, please send me the necessary forms, etc.

Yours faithfully,
Sd/-
Ramsay Mann
14, Residency Road,
California

Date ________

Reply to the Above

Date __________

Mr. Ramsay Mann,
Residency Road,
California.

Sir,

Reference to your letter, we have the pleasure in enclosing a Savings Account Opening Form. Please fill up the same and call on us in person to append your specimen signatures.

Yours faithfully,
Sd/-
Post Master

Encl :- Savings Account Form.

Forwarding a Cheque for Credit in the Savings Account

Date ___________

The Post Master,
Bandung.

Dear Sir,

I am enclosing Cheque No. 131428 dated 12th Oct., 19____, for Rs. 108.

Please collect the same on my behalf and credit the proceeds to my savings account No. 183848.

Thank you.

Yours faithfully,
Sd/-
Amir Srikerta

Asking for Return of TMO/Regd. letter

IMPERIAL CENT COMPANY
M.G. Road,
London.

16th Oct., 19____

The Post Master,
G.P.O.,
Glasgow.

Dear Sir,

We sent you a TMO/Reg. Letter on 10th October, 19____, in the name of Mr. Ron Jenkins, our Sales Representative. Since Mr. Jenkins has returned to London this morning and would be here for another one month, please return the TMO/Regd. Letter per return of post.

Thank you.

Yours faithfully,
For Imperial Cent Co.,
Sd/-

Encashment of a Postal Order

NAPLES BOTTLING CO.,
High Road,
Liverpool.

The Post Master,
High Road,
Liverpool.

Dear Sir,

We are sending through bearer, our representative Mr. Ray Jones Postal orders worth £100 duly signed and stamped.

Please pay the amount to our representative. His attested signatures appear below.

Thank you.

Yours faithfully,
For Naples bottling Co.,
Sd/-
Partner

Attested Signatures of Mr. Ray Jones.

Asking for the Issue of a Business Reply Permit

LAWRENCE INDUSTRIES
City Centre,
Manchester.

The Post Master,
City Centre,
Manchester.

Dear Sir,

In order to expand our business further, we wish to send Reply-Pad envelopes to our clients. We, therefore, request you to please issue us the necessary Business Reply Permit.

Thank you.

Yours faithfully,
For Lawrence Industries,
Sd/-
Manager
14, City Centre
Manchester.

Reply to the Above

From: Postmaster,
City Centre, Manchester.
To: M/s. Lawrence Industries,
14, City Centre,
Manchester.

Sub:— B.R. Cards and Envelopes-Issue/Renewal of permit.

Ref.:— Your letter No. OF 46, dated 11th June, 19____

1. M/s. Lawrence Industries. 14, City Centre, London are hereby permitted, to post B.R. Cards and envelopes under permit No. 1763 for further period of one year with effect from 22-11____ to 21-11____.
2. The fee of £100 (Pound one Hundred only) has been deposited by the applicant to the Head Post Office.
3. The permit No. 1763 is enclosed for delivery to the applicant under receipt. An entry regarding the same may be made in the relevant register.
4. Attention is also invited to clause 54 B (4) of P&T Guide Part-1. In case the renewal of permit is desired the holder must submit his application well before the expiry of the period of currency, failing which his article should be treated as ordinary unpaid mail after the date of expiry of the permit and until the issues of a permit. No period of grace will in any case by allowed.

Sd/- (Post Master)

Instructions Regarding Business Reply Permit

Business Reply Card/Envelope/Label

Postage will be
paid by the
addressee

No. Postage stamp
is necessary if posted
in England

Permit No.:—
London Head Post Office

To
Messrs Anybody,
XZY Street,
London-1

Business Reply Cards, Envelopes and labels must be on the address side, either printed thereon or on a label affixed thereto (*a*) the printed name and address to the permit-holder to whom the card or envelope is to be delivered, (*b*) the permit number, (*c*) the name of the post office issuing the permit, (*d*) two thick vertical lines in black or any other colour near the right hand edge, (*e*) the words "Business Reply Card", "Business Reply Envelope", or "Business Reply Label" as the case may be, (*f*) the words "No postage stamp is necessary if posted in UK", and (*g*) the words "Postage will be paid by the addressee". Sufficient space should be left for post making at the top of the card or envelope. The design suggested for postcards above may be adopted. A permit-holder may incorporate in any advertisement issued by him in a newspaper or other publication a special design containing the printed entries herein-before specified with a view to its being used as a business Reply Label and affixed to a card or envelope.

A "Business Reply Card" shall not be folded, cut or otherwise altered.

Business Reply Cards may be sent out as reply portions of double postcards or may be enclosed with the order matter, but Business Reply Envelopes must be enclosed with the other matter.

When Business Reply Cards and Envelopes are returned to the office of origin, they will be delivered to the person for whom they are intended on payment of the Postage chargeable thereon.

Business Reply Cards and Envelopes cannot be sent marked for Express Delivery.

The provisions of the Clause 107 will apply, so far as they apply to Post Cards.

Another Reply (Negative)

From: Post Master,
City Centre,
Manchester.

18th March, 19____

To

Messers Lawrence Industries,
14, City Centre,
Manchester.

Dear Sirs,

With reference to your letter dated 11th Jan. 19____ the report of our Inspector does not justify the issue of a Business Reply Permit at this stage.

Yours faithfully,
Sd/-
Post Master.

Missing of VPP Receipts

POPULAR BOOK SHOP
New Valley Road,
Glasgow.

23rd Dec., 19____

The Post Master,
Glasgow.

Sub: VP Journal Receipts

Dear Sir,

We have today observed that VP Journal allotted to us does not contain receipts from 311 to 320. And from the binding of the VP Journal it appears that through an oversight these numbers were not printed.

Please note and record the same.

Yours faithfully,
For Popular Book Shop,
Sd/-
Manager

Complaint Regarding Non-Receipt of VP Money / Article

IMPERIAL CENT CO.
M.G. Road,
London.

The Post Master,
M.G. Road,
London.

7th March, 19____

Sub: VP Article 1402 of 9-1-19____ for £70 in the name of M/s. Delta Voyage, 14, Hoyle Road, Leeds.

Dear Sir,

The above VP letter was sent through your post office on 1-1-19____. Although more than two months have since passed, we have neither received the payment nor the VP letter back. We shall appreciate your looking into the matter immediately.

Thank you.

Yours faithfully,
For Imperial Cent Company,
Sd/-
Manager

N.B. — A search fee of £0.50 is enclosed as per a postal stamp of the same value.

Reply to the Above

From : Post Master
M.G. Road,
London.

To
M/s. Imperial Cent Company,
M.G. Road,
London.

16th March 19____

Sub: VP Article No. 1402 dated 1-1-19____ for £270 in the name of M/s Delta Voyage, 14 Hoyle Road, Leeds.

Dear Sir,

Reference your letter dated 7th March, 19___, on the subject referred to above, please note that the article was returned to you on 11-1-19____, as the party concerned did not release the same.

Yours faithfully,
Sd/-
For Post Master.

Complaint regarding Non-Receipt of Packets by a Foreign Client

IMPERIAL CENT. CO.
M.G. Road,
London.

10th March, 19____

The Post Master,
M.G. Road,
London.

Subject: — Reg. Packets — SINGAPORE.

Dear Sir,

Four regd. packets were sent through you on the 12th October, 19____, in the name of M/s Stephens, Shrangoon Road, Singapore vide Receipt Nos. 131, 132, 133 and 134.

Although more than five months have since passed, our clients have not yet received the goods. Will you kindly look into the matter immediately?

A search fee of £2 in the form of postal stamps is enclosed.

Yours faithfully,
For Imperial Cent Co.
Sd/-
Manager

Encl:— Postal stamps for £2

Applying for Registration of the Magazine for Concessional Rates.

LITERARY BOOK DEPOT
Grant Street,
London.

16th November, 19____

The Post Master,
London.

Dear Sir,

We have now released the first issue of our monthly magazine entitled 'LITERAL DIGEST'. Two copies of the same are sent herewith for your information and record. Please grant us the permission to send the same at concessional rates.

Yours faithfully,
For Literal Book Dept,
Sd/-
Proprietor.

Reply to Above

UK POSTS AND TELEGRAPHS DEPARTMENT
London.

To,

The Literary Book Depot,
Grant Street,
London.

No. Tech/Regn. — 83 London dated 13-12-19____

Subject:— Registration of 'Literal Digest' for posting on concessional rates.

Dear Sir,

I am directed to refer to your letter dated 16th November, 19____, on the subject mentioned above and to say that the form and nature of the contents of your magazine do not confirm to the provisions of Section 9(2) of the UK P & T Act and the rule made thereunder read with clause 132 of the P.O. Guide, Part I. It is, therefore, regretted that your magazine cannot be registered for posting on concessional rates.

Yours faithfully,
Sd/-
Asst. Director of Postal Services

19
Payments—Collections

Informing a Client Regarding Payment of Promissory Note

NEW ORIENT COMPANY
Strafford.

19th December, 19____

Dear Sir,

We regret very much to write that we have not yet received the payment of our Promissory Note (P.N.) which fell due on 9-12-19____.

Please intimate us the date when you returned the (P.N.) so that we may write to your bankers accordingly.

Thank you.

Yours faithfully,
For New Orient Company,
Sd/-

Requesting a Client to make Cash Payment (Letter of Authority for Payment)

KELLY & SONS
Vanconver.

17th December, 19____

N/40/79

M/s. Jones & Jones,
Vanconver.

Dear Sir,

This is to request you to please make cash payment of our Bills No. 5485 and 5545 for US $219 and 112 respectively to the bearer of this letter.

Mr. Martin Chang, our sales representative.

Thank you.

Yours faithfully,
For Jones & Jones
Sd/-

Informing Suppliers for Non-Deduction of Credit from the Bill

AVTAR SINGH & CO.
The Mall,
Chicago.

M/s. Parry Mason & Sons,
River Avenue,
Los Angeles.

Dear Sir,

You have sent us a V.P.P. for US $250.00 in execution of our order No. 5510 dated 22-8-19____.

We had returned to you goods worth US $75.00 and this amount was to be adjusted in our bill against the above order as mentioned therein. You have, however not adjusted this amount of US $75.00.

We are, therefore, returning your V.P.P. Kindly send us a fresh V.P.P. after deducting US $75.00 that the RR is returned.

The goods are incurring demurrage. Please also deduct US $50.00 on this account while resubmitting the RR by VPP.

Thank you.

Yours faithfully,
For Avtar Singh & Co.,
Sd/-
Partner

Reply to the Above

PARRY MASON & SONS
River Avenue,
Los Angeles.

19-9-19____

M/s. Avtar Singh & Co.,
The Mall ,
Chicago.

Dear Sirs,

We thank you for your letter dated 14-9-19____. The gross value of the goods returned by you is US $100, which through an oversight the gross value deducted from your Bill No. 3077 is US $66. This has happened through an oversight only.

The gross value of US $100 *i.e.,* US $60 net has now been deducted from your current VPL and you are requested to please release the same immediately.

Thank you.

Yours faithfully,
For Parry Mason & Sons,
Sd/-

Complaint Regarding Difference in Discount

IMPERIAL GLASS COMPANY
Southempton.

22nd September, 19____

No. IGC/9/439
Messrs Fine Glass,
Market Arcade,
London.

Dear Mr. Charles,

Re: Your Invoice No. 9282 dated 20-9-19_____.

We are surprised to receive your above Invoice allowing only 40% discount instead of 45% and we refer to our letter No. IGC/9/72/432 dated 14-9-19____, wherein we have complained that instead of allowing 45%, you have allowed only 40%.

This time we are requesting you to call back the P.N. and send correct bill after allowing difference of discount on your invoice No. 9005 dated 7-9-19____.

Hope you will do accordingly and your expeditions action is solicited.

Thank you.

Yours faithfully,
For Imperial Glass Co.,
Sd/-
M. Engineer.

Reply to the Above

FINE GLASS
Market Arcade,
London.

26th Sept., 19____

Dear Mr. Engineer,

I thank you for your letter No. IGC/9/439 dated the 22nd inst.

Since the normal maximum discount allowed is 40% through an oversight this discount has been deducted in our Bill No. 9005 and 9282. The gross value of the two Bills is £2500 on which an additional 6% discount is payable to you.

In order to avoid accounting complications, I am enclosing herewith our Cheque No. 139924 dated the 25th Sept., 19____ for £125 towards the difference in both the bills. This brings the accounts up-to-date and you may release the P.N. accordingly.

With best wishes and kindest regards.

Yours Sincerely,
For Fine Glass,
Sd/-
M.K. Charles
Managing Partner

Encl: Cheque.
Sh. M. Engineer
Imperial Glass Company,
Southampton.

Statement of Account

CAPITAL INSTALLATIONS LTD.,
Detroit.

Date 21st Jan, 19____

Ref. No. P/176/74

Messrs Jamie Sons,
1st Cross Street,
New York.

Dear Sirs,

We are submitting below a statement of Account for the months of November and December, 19____.

S.No.	*Bill No.*	*Date*	*Amount US$*
1	31	4-1-19-	790.00
2	79	7-11-19-	1,011.00
3	127	16-11-19-	683.00
4	189	30-11-19-	2,775.00
5	201	16-12-19-	3,703.00
6	222	17-12-19-	1,121.00
			10,083.00

As all the bills are now due, we shall be glad to have your draft for US $10,083 per return of post.

Thank you.

Yours faithfully,
For Capital Installations,
Sd/-

Reply to the above pointing out an Error

JAMIE SONS
1st Cross Street,
New York.

28th Jan, 19____

Messrs Capital Installations Ltd.,
Detroit.

Dear Sirs,

We thank you for your letter dated 21st Jan., 19 ____.

While checking our accounts, we observe that the Bill No. 189 dated 30th Nov. for US $2775.00 has neither been received by us nor have we placed any order for the goods. We have therefore, deducted this amount and a cheque for US $7,308 towards the full payment of other bills in enclosed.

Please acknowledge receipt.

Thank you.

Yours faithfully,
For Jamine Sons,
Sd/-

Encl: Cheque

Requesting for Extension of the Credit Period

JAMIES SONS
1st Cross Street,
New York.

28th Jan., 19____

Messrs Capital Installations Ltd.
Detroit

Dear Sirs,

We thank you for your letter dated 21st Jan., 19____ informing us regarding the due payments of US $10,083.

As you are aware, there had been heavy rain in USA in November and December, the business as a whole has received a heavy setback and it is only for the last one week that the business has started improving. Under the circumstances, we are not in a position to make any payments right now. However, we assure you that we shall be in a position to remit the amount in full in about a month's time. We hope you will bear with us until then.

In the meanwhile we thank you once again and assure you of our best co-operation always.

Yours faithfully,
For Jamie Sons,
Sd/-

Making Part Payment

XYZ & CO.
Water Front
New York

18th Nov. 19____

Messrs ABC & Co.
The Mall,
Florida.

Dear Sirs,

We take pleasure in enclosing our Cheque for US $8,000 towards part payment of your Bill No. 171 dated 17th July, 19____. We shall arrange to send the balance payment of US $6000 by the month-end.

Thank you.

Yours faithfully,
For XYZ & Co.,
Sd/-

Encl: Cheque

A Good Reminder for Payment

JOHNSON & SONS
California

18th June, 19____

Messrs Ansari Bros.,
Abid Road,
California U.S.A.

Dear Sirs,

This is intended merely as a friendly reminder on your due account of US $500 which we believe you have overlooked.

Now that it has been brought to your attention, we are sure you will want to bring you account up-to-date.

If by any chance your Cheque is already in the mail, please disregard this reminder and accept our thanks.

Yours faithfully,
For Johnson & Sons,
Sd/-

Returning Excess Payment Received through an Oversight

GOODWILL PUBLISHING HOUSE
18, Mollins Street,
London.

9th Aug., 19____

Herbeht & Co.,
Cliff Road,
Dover 329.

Dear Sirs,

We thank you for your letter No. AC/J/677, dated the 20th inst.

We regret very much to say that through an oversight a sum of £100 was drawn in excess against our Bill No. 6488. We are enclosing herewith our cheque for £100 to square up the accounts.

Inconvenience caused to you is very much regretted.

Thank you,

Yours faithfully,
For New Light Publishers,
Sd/-

Encl: Cheque for US $100.

Enclosing Draft/Cheque

Phones: 73822, 64312

UNIVERSAL PEN STALL
The Mall,
Chicago.

Dated 16-12-19____

Messrs Woodcock Stores,
New York.

Dear Sirs,

We are enclosing herewith the Cheque No. KP-0077/48/762/69 dated 16-12-19__ for US $113.34 drawn in your favour on City Bank Broadway,

New York in full payment of the following invoices. Please credit the amount to our account and acknowledge receipt at an early date.

Thank you.

Yours faithfully,
For Universal Pen Stall
Sd/-

Encl: draft

Bill No.	Date	Amount
236	5-12-83	US $113.24

Reply to the Above

WOODCOCK STORES
New Complex,
New York 3292

23rd Dec., 19____

The Universal Pen Stall,
The Mall,
Chicago.

Dear Sirs,

We thank you for your letter dated 16-12-19____ together with a cheque for US $113.34 in full and final settlement of our bill No. 236 dated 5-12-19____. We have pleasure in enclosing our current order at an early date.

Thank you.

Yours faithfully,
For Woodcock Stores
Sd/-

Encl: As above.

Informing the Client Regarding Return of Documents and Re-despatch of the same through VPL

MODERN INDUSTRIES
Bandung

N/40/71
M/s. The Universal Traders,
Old Market.
Surabaya.

Dear Sirs,

In compliance with your order dated 12-10-19_____, we sent the goods per passenger train and forwarded the documents through V.P.L.

The documents were received back unclaimed by you and presuming that this might have happened through an oversight only, we sent the same again through V.P.L.

We now regret very much to note that the V.P.L. has been received back for the second time.

As a special case we are sending the V.P.L. once again and shall very much appreciate your releasing the same on presentation in our mutual interest.

We may, however, mentioned here that in case the documents are received back this time also, we shall have no choice except to call back the parcel. In that case we shall execute no orders of yours in future unless full expenses of this order together with a sufficient advance are sent to us.

Further, please note that our Sales Representative, Mr. U.S. Hussain, is on tour and shall call on you by the 3rd week of this month.

In the meanwhile we thank you once again and assure you of our best co-operation always.

Thank you.

Yours faithfully,
For Modern Industries,
Sd/-
Manger.

Regarding Return of Promissory Note from the Bank

ABDULLA SHOE CO.
Penang.

M/s. New Book House Ltd.
Mount Road,
Kuala Lumpur.

Dear Sirs,

It is much to our surprise that our Promissory Note for US $296.09 has been received as unclaimed by you on due date.

We are sending the PN under VPL for Rs. 300.69 and shall very much appreciate your releasing the same on presentation.

Needless to say our general terms are strictly cash. This is only on the request of our Sales Representative Mr. S. Abid, that documents were sent to you at sight. We do hope that you will keep this preferential advantage to you in your mind and will release the documents immediately.

Thank you.

Yours faithfully,
For Abdullah Shoe Co.,
Sd/-

Lawyer's Notice Regarding Payment

Phones: Off.: 225200 Resi: 220983
40-D, Pent Lane
Hong Kong
22nd Jan., 19____

MUKHTIAR HUSSAIN
Advocate
M/s. M.N. Book Stall,
Cionge, Hong Kong.

Dear Sirs,

Under instructions from and on behalf of my clients, M.N. Book Stall, Cionge, Hong Kong, I write as follows:—

1. That in compliance with the order placed by you with my client at Delhi, my client supplied you books worth US $302.44 on credit.

2. That my client has undergone an expense of US $10.00 on account of the correspondence and V.P.L., charges in respect of the aforesaid consignment which is also payable by you.

3. That according to the custom and usage of the market, you are liable to pay interest to my client @ US $1 P.M. and now a sum of US $20.00 as interest and US $302.44 as Principal totalling US $322.44 is due from you which you have not paid in spite of repeated requests and demands.

I, therefore, do hereby call upon you to pay the aforesaid amount of US $322.44 along with US $5.80 as costs of this notice, within a week of the receipt of this notice by you, to my client failing which my client shall be constrained to file a suit for the recovery of the same against you and in that event you will be liable for the costs and expenses of my client.

Copy of the notice has been kept.

Yours faithfully,
Sd/-
Advocate.

20
Banking Correspondence

Opening a Savings Bank Account

Date : ______

The Manager,
United Bank,
Bank Street,
London.

Dear Sir,

As I intend to open a Savings Bank Account with you, I request you, to send me the necessary forms for specimen signatures, etc.

Thank you.

Yours faithfully,
Sd/- Amber Raj,
31/1, Pon Lone
London

Reply to the Above

ENELPEE

UNITED BANK
Bank Street
London

Ref. No:-

Mr. Amber Raj,
31/1, Pon Lone,
London.

Dear Sir,

We thank you for your letter dated _____.

We are enclosing the necessary forms for opening a Savings Bank

Account with us. Please fill up the same and call on us in person to give your specimens signatures.

Assuring you of our best services,

Yours faithfully,
Sd/-
Manager

Encl: As above

Letter for Opening a Current Account

Grams :—
Tel.:—

GENERAL TRADERS
Milton Road,
Liverpool.

Ref. No:—
The Manager,
Lloyd Bank Ltd.,
Liverpool.

Dear Sir,

As we wish to open a Current Account in your bank, we request you to please send us necessary forms for the same.

Thank you.

Yours faithfully,
For General Traders,
Sd/-
Manger/Partner.

Reply to the Above

LLOYDS BANK LIMITED
King's Avenue
Liverpool

Date: ____

Ref. No. ____
M/s. General Traders,
Milton Road,
Liverpool.

Dear Sirs,

We thank you for your letter No. ____ dated ____.

We have pleasure in enclosing the necessary forms for opening a Current Account.

We may add here that all such persons who wish to operate the bank account, should call on us in person to give their specimen signatures.

Assuring you of our best services.

Yours faithfully,
Sd/-
For Manager

Encls: As above

Requesting the Bank to Issue a Cheque Book

SULTANA & COMPANY
Singapore

Dated 18th Oct., 19____

Ref. No.:— 1/73-74
The Manager,
Bank of Tokyo,
Singapore.

Dear Sir,

This is to request you to please deliver a cheque book containing 100 cheques to Mr. Yang Lee, our Accountant and the bearer of this letter.

Mr. Yang Lee signature is attested herewith.

Thank you.

Yours faithfully,
For Sultana & Company,
Sd/-
Managing Partner

Sd/-
(Yang Lee)

Enquiring about the Bank Balance

SULTANA & COMPANY
Singapore

10th Nov., 19____

Ref. No.: 2/73-74
The Manager,
Bank of Tokyo,
Singapore

Sub :— Current Account — Sultana & Company.

Dear Sir,

Please inform the credit balance of the above account to the bearer of this letter.

Thank you.

Yours faithfully,
For Sultana & Company,
Sd/-
Managing Partner.

Letter to the Bank for Opening a Second Account

ANTONIA PUBLISHERS
(Publishers of Text-Books)
Ali Razak Road
Kuala Lumpur

13th Sept., 19____

Ref. No. :— A/72

The Manager,
Hong Kong Bank,
Ali Razak Road,
Kuala Lumpur.

Dear Sir,

We enclose a Draft No. AL 160041 dated 1st Sept., 19____. for US $25,000. The proceeds of the draft may please be credited to a new account which we wish to open in your Bank and which will be called ANTONIAS AGENCIES ACCOUNT. In case any fresh forms are to be signed, please send the same to us.

Thank you.

Yours faithfully,
For Antonia Publishers
Sd/-
Manager

Stopping Payment of a Cheque

MAINUDDIN BROTHERS
Jakarta

To,

The Manager,
New Hong Kong Bank,
Jakarta.

Dear Sir,

We have been informed by our clients, Messrs Garments P.T., that they have lost our cheque No. BD 167323 of 15th instant for US $200. Please stop payment of the same and inform us per return of post of your having done so, that we may issue a fresh cheque.

Thank you.

Yours faithfully,
For Mainuddin Bros.,
Sd/-
Manager

Reply to the Above

NEW HONG KONG BANK
Jakarta

Dear Sirs,

With reference to your letter No. ____ dated ____, please note that the payment of the cheque under reference has been stopped.

Assuring you of our best services.

Yours faithfully,
Sd/-
Manager.

Depositing a Cheque

To,

The Manager,
Asia Bank,

Bandung.

Dear Sir,

We are enclosing herewith a cheque for US $1373.12 which please release on our behalf and credit and proceeds to our account.

Thank you.

Yours faithfully,
Sd/-
Wholesale Agencies,
Bandung

Note:— However, the modern practice of depositing a cheque is through the Bank Deposit Slips.

Reply to the Above

ASIA BANK
Bandung.

4th, Jan., 19____

Ref. No.:— 274
Messrs. Wholesale Agencies,
Bandung.

Dear Sirs,

We thank you for your letter No. ____ dated ____ together with a cheque for US $1373.12.

The proceeds of your cheque have been credited to your account after deducting a sum of US $2.75 towards the clearing charges.

Thank you.

Yours faithfully,
Sd/-
Manger

Usual Form of a Bank informing his Client Regarding his Account having been Debited or Credited

NATIONAL & GRINDLAYS BANK LTD.
Long Circus
USA

10th April, 19_____

Messrs ......

Dear Sir/Sirs,

The Manager presents his compliments and begs to advise that your..... account has been credited/debited with US $ ...... on account of ....

Yours faithfully,
For National & Grindlays Bank Ltd.,
Sd/-
For Manager

Requesting for a Pass Book

Grams:

AMERICAN TRADERS
Shirangun Road,
Singapore.

Date : _____

Ref. No.

The Agent,
Bank of Tokyo,
Singapore.

Sub:— Pass Book — American Traders Ltd.,

Dear Sir,

Please deliver to the bearer, our Pass Book of the above account.

Thank you.

Yours faithfully,
For American Traders
Sd/-

Another Letter Regarding a Pass Book

Grams:

AMERICAN TRADERS
Shirangun Road,
Singapore.

10th Oc., 19____
Ref. No.: AT/16

The Agent,
Bank of Tokyo,
Singapore.

(For Personal Attention of the Agent)

Sub:— Pass Book

Dear Sir,

It is much to our surprise that despite our requests on telephone, as also in writing, we have not received the Pass Book so far.

The old Pass Book up to 31st March was returned to you about three months back with a request to issue us yearly Pass Books from 1st April to 31st March for the convenience of our accounts.

We now request you once again to please give us our old Pass Book up to 31st March and a fresh Pass Book from 1st April up-to-date.

Thanking you,

Yours faithfully,
For American Traders,
Sd/-

Reply to the Above

THE BANK OF TOKYO
Singapore

12th Oct., 19____

Telegraphic Address: Bank
Telephone: 816438.

In reply please quote,
No. 113/73-74,

Messrs American Traders,
Shirangun Road,
Singapore.

Sub: Pass Book

Dear Sirs,

I thankfully acknowledge the receipt of your letter No. AT/16 dated 12th Oct., 19____

On checking the matter with our Current Account Section, I am informed that they have not been able to trace the Pass Book and it is for this reason that the matter has been delayed. May I, therefore, request you to please check up once again if by any chance the Pass Book is lying at your end? In any case, I assure you that the job will be done within two/three days after receipt of your reply.

Thank you.

Yours faithfully,
Sd/-
Agent

Forwarding a Copy of Partnership Deed

INTERNATIONAL TEXTILES
Karachi

13th Nov., 19____

Ref.:— 1371
The Manager,
Bank of America,
Karachi.

Dear Sir,

We are sending through bearer a copy of Partnership Deed duly attested. This was not supplied at the time of opening the account.

Thanking you.

Yours faithfully,
For International Textiles
Sd/-

Informing the Bank Regarding Inclusion of Another Partner in the Firm

NATIONAL BOOK CLUB
Penang

29th March, 19____

Ref. No. 14
The Manager,
British Bank,
Penang.

Dear Sir,

This is to bring to your information that we are taking one more partner (Mr. Lin Pin Chou S/o Mr. Lieu Jae Chou) in our partnership from 1-4-19____.

The new account would stand in the same Name and Style of NATIONAL BOOK CLUB, and would be operated individually/jointly by

1. ABDUL RAZAK
2. ABID RAZAK
3. LIN PIN CHOU

The old account standing in the name of NATIONAL BOOK CORPORATION, may please be transferred to the new account of the same name.

Thank you.

Yours faithfully,
For National Book Club
Sd/-

Reply to the Above

URGENT

Grams: COBANK

Tel : 583828

BRITISH BANK
Singapore

30th March, 19____

Ref. No.— 209
Messrs National Book Club,
Singapore.

Dear Sirs,

We thank you for your letter No. 14 dated 29th March, 19____.

Please call on us (all the partners) in person on the morning of 1st April to sign fresh papers.

Thanking you.

Yours faithfully,
Sd/-
For Manager

Informing the Bank of Honour All the Cheques of the Previous Partnership

NATIONAL BOOK CLUB
Singapore

1st April, 19____

Ref. No. 24
The Manager,
British Bank.,
Singapore.

Dear Sir,

This is to request you to please honour all our cheques issued before 31st March 19____, and debit the amount to our new account which we have today in the name of new partnership.

Thank you.

Yours faithfully,
For National Book Club
Sd/-
1. Abdul Pazak
2. Abid Razak
3. Lin Pin Chou

Note: This letter must be signed by all the partners of new partnership.

Sending Documents to the Party's Bankers

Registered A.D.

DELUXE SOAP COMPANY
Jalan Amin
Jakarta
Indonesia

14th Nov., 19____

Ref. No.— Bank/211
The Manager,
Karya Bank,
Jakarta.

Dear Sir,

We enclose herewith:—

1. Bill No. 16, dated 13th Nov., 19_____, for US $1000; and
2. PWB No. 11731 dated 13th Nov., 19____

Please deliver these documents to Messrs Hussain & Co., Jakarta against full payment.

All bank charges may please be collected from the party concerned and the net amount of the documents sent to us by a Bank Draft on realisation.

Thank you.

Yours faithfully,
For Deluxe Soap Company
Sd/-

Encl: As Above

Sending Documents with Promissory Note

Registered A.D.
DELUXE SOAP COMPANY
Jalan Amin
Jakarta

17th Nov., 19____

Ref. No. Bank/144
The Manager,
National Bank,
Bandung.

Dear Sir,

We are enclosing herewith :—

1. Bill No. 23, dated 16th Nov., 19____, for US $1,660;
2. PWB No. 14732, dated 15th Nov., 19____; and
3. Promissory Note at 60 days sight.

Please deliver the above documents to Messrs Lubis & Company, against acceptance to pay a sum of US $1,660 (Dollar One thousand six hundred and sixty only) at 60 days sight from the date of acceptance.

The date of maturity of documents may kindly be intimated to us at your earliest.

Thank you.

Yours faithfully,
For Deluxe Soap Co.,
Sd/-

Encl : As above.

Sending a Promissory Note to the Bank Left Inadvertently

DELUXE SOAP COMPANY
Jalan Amin
Jakarta (Indonesia)

18th Nov., 19____

Ref. No. Bank/257

The Manager,
National Bank,
Bandung.

Sub:— Our Bill No. 23, dated 16th Nov., 19____, for US $1,660/
M/s Lubis & Co.,

Dear Sir,

With further reference to our letter No. Bank/244, dated the 17th November, 19____, we are sending herewith a Promissory for US $1,660 which was not sent with the documents through an oversight.

Yours faithfully,

For De-Luxe Soap Co.,
Sd/-

Encl - PN

Letter from the Bank to a Drawee for Acceptance of Promissory Note

Gram:

Tel.:

UNDER CERTIFICATE OF POSTING
NATIONAL BANK
Bandung

27th Nov., 19____

Ref. No.: PNB/A/17

Messrs Lubis & Co.,
Jalan Barat,
Bandung.

Dear Sir,

Re: P.N. for US $1,600.

Endorsed by Messrs Deluxe Soap Company, Jakarta, please call on us to accept the same.

Yours faithfully,
Sd/-
Accountant

Letter from the Bank to a Drawer Regarding Due Date of the Promissory Note

Grams:
Tel.

NATIONAL BANK
Bandung

6th Dec., 19____

Ref. No. PNB/H/1603

Messrs Deluxe Soap Company,
Jalan Amin,
Jakarta.

Sub:— Promissory Note For US $1,600 in the name of Messrs Topan & Co.

Dear Sir,

With reference to the above, please note that the PN has been accepted by the party and the payment of the same falls due on 4th February, 19____.

Assuring you of our best services.

Yours faithfully,
Sd/-
For Manager

Regarding Despatch of Documents to the Local Bank for Forwarding the same to the Drawee's bank

ROXY FURNITURE
Ocean View,
Florida.

Ref. No. 111/73-74

The Manager,
City Bank Ltd.,
Ocean View,
Florida.

Dear Sir,

We are enclosing—

1. Bill No. 158, dated 9th August 19____, for US $227.65.
2. Goods Receipt No. 30102 from Patiala Roadways.

These documents may please to sent to Express Bank, California, for collection from M/s. Western Stores, California.

All bank charges are to be collected from the party concerned and net proceeds of the documents credited to our account on realisation.

Documents* if uncleared up to 3rd September, 19____, may please be returned to us without seeking any further instructions.

Thank you.

Yours faithfully,
For Roxy Furniture
Sd/-
Encl: As Above

*Alternatively substitute "In case the documents are not cleared up to 3rd September, 19____, please intimate to us. In no case the documents should be returned to us before consulting us".

Note: Generally the above documents are delivered to the local bankers by a representative, personally. Printed Forms on the subject are also available with the Banks.

Letter from a Bank Enclosing Remittances

WESTERN BANK
Avenue Road
Boston

15th Nov., 19____

Ref No. EE/BC 83

M/s. Larsen Engineering,
Lincoln Avenue,
New York.

Ref: Your Letter No. 1683, dated 10th October, 19____.

Dear Sirs,

We enclose remittance of US $830.00 by our draft No. 816731 dated 13th November, 19____, on Lincoln Avenue Branch made up as per Memo at the foot receipt of which please acknowledge.

Memo

No	Particulars	Amount US	$
816731	Your letter No. 1683 —M/s Cordial Traders	830	00
		830	00

Yours faithfully,
Sd/-
Manager

Encl: One.

Returning Uncleared Documents

REGISTERED
STATE BANK OF FLORIDA
Florida

VPP for US $5.00

Returned Cheque Remittance Memo

8th March, 19____

M/s. Wilson & Sons,
Main Road,
Kentucky.

Dear Sirs,

Being unable to obtain payment of the enclosed documents for US

$373.22 on Watson and Johnson Brothers for the reason given on the memo attached hereto, we beg to return it to you.

Yours faithfully,
Sd/-
Accountant/Manager

Encl: 1. Bill No. 1673

2. R/R 134123

Form of a Memo indicating reasons for Returning Documents

CITY BANK OF USA
New York

Dated : _____

Cheque No. 048321 for US $8744.00

MEMORANDUM

The above Cheque is returned for reason(s) No (s) — 14

1. Payee's endorsement required.
2. Payee's endorsement irregular.
3. Payee's endorsement in language other than English or the local regional language requires Bank's confirmation.
4. Cheque irregularly drawn.
5. Collecting Bank's confirmation requires Clearing Bank's authentication.
6. Crossed to two Banks.
7. Specially crossed to..... Bank.
8. Not arranged for.
9. Refer to drawer.
10. Full cover not received.
11. Exceeds arrangements.
12. Effects not cleared, please present again.
13. Drawer's signature required.
14. Drawer's signature differs with the specimen on record.
15. Drawer's signature incomplete.
16. Withdrawals from account stopped by drawer's death/insolvency/ lunacy.

17. Payment stopped by the drawer.
18. Operation on the account suspended under Court's strain Order/ Attachment Order of the Income Tax Authorities.
19. Amount in words and figures differ.
20. Alteration in date/figures/words requires the drawer's signature.
21. Cheque/Pay Order/Draft is mutilated/postdated/out of date.
22. Cheque/Pay Order/Draft is mutilated—requires Bank's guarantee.
23. Cross entry (a) incorrect
    (b) required
    (c) illegible

(*Note:* Cross entry refers to protective cross amount)

24. No Account.
25. Account closed. Account transferred to ... Branch.
26. No advice.
27. Amount/Name of Payee differs from that on advice.
28. Wrongly delivered.
29. Drawing contrary to 'Savings Bank Rules'.
30. Not payable at....
31. Cheque contains extraneous matter.
32. Drawee Bank's funds with the ..... (name of the sponsor bank) insufficient.
33. Payee's receipt incomplete.
34. E.C.D. From A, 7 approved by the Exchange Control required.
35. Drawer's signature/authority to operate on the Account not received at this office.
36. Payee's thumb impression requires attestation by a Magistrate under his Court Seal or by collecting bankers.

For Government Instruments

37. Not payable till 1st proximo.
38. Refund order is not transferable.
39. Date/place of payment required to the completed/mentioned under full signature of the Drawing/Refund Officer.
40. Government drafts are not transferable.

41. Clearing stamp of date required.

(*Regd. Office* : 14, Hewitt Road, New Jersey)
NATIONAL BANK LTD.,

Date : 1-7-19_____

Sd/-
Manager/Agent.

Bank Forwarding Documents to another Bank for Collection/Registered

BANK OF TOKYO
Great Eastern Avenue,
New York.

Date : 1st Oct., 19____

Post Box No. 2571
In reply please quote
No. ANT/17

Dear Sirs,

We beg to send you herewith the undernoted Bill for collection and should be obliged if you would kindly send the proceeds to us on realisation by a credit note/draft on New Delhi.

Please follow the instructions marked X:

INSTRUCTIONS

1. Deliver documents against Payment/Acceptance.
2. Collect our commission US $3.00 and your commission from the drawees.
3. Deduct your commission from the proceeds.
4. Charge interest @ ....
5. Advise nonacceptance/non-payment.
6. If not paid within 10th October on presentation please return the bill.
7. Please collect Goods Tax from 'C'.
8. Kindly advice the due date.

Yours faithfully,
Sd/-

O.B.C. OR	D.D. No.	M.T.R./R.R. No.	INVOICE No.	DRAWEE	AMOUNT US$
9/210		17384	273	M/s Roberts & Robbins	400.00

Copy to:— M/s John Gill & Sons.

Letter to a Bank for the Overdraft Facilities

ZAIDULLAH & SONS
Main Road,
Karachi.

19th, Nov., 19____

Ref. No. 17

The Manager,
Co-operative Bank Ltd.,
Karachi.

Ref : Our Current Account No. 70

Dear Sir,

We wish to have overdraft facilities for which we are prepared to deposit with your State Government Securities of the face value of US $8000.

We shall very much appreciate your sending us the necessary forms for signature.

In case any further particulars are required, the undersigned would be glad to call on you personally.

Thank you.

Yours faithfully,
For Zaidullah & Sons.
Sd/-
Partner

Reply to Above

CO-OPERATIVE BANK LTD.
Karachi.

Date 24th Nov., 19____

Ref. No. ODF/A/73-74

Messrs. Zaidullah & Sons,
Main Road,
Karachi.

Dear Sirs,

We thank you for your letter No. 17 dated 19th Nov., 19____, regarding overdraft facilities.

Necessary forms and promissory note are enclosed herewith. Please fill the same and sign on places marked in red ink. The Government Securities duly endorsed in our favour along with the forms may then be sent to us to enable us to give you the necessary Overdraft facilities.

Yours faithfully,
Sd/-
Manager

Complaint to the Bank Regarding a Mistake in the Account

CENTRAL INDUSTRIES LTD.
Hong Kong

Date 11-3 -19____

Ref. No. _____

The Manager,
The Commercial Bank.,
Kuala Lumpur.

Dear Sir,

Current — Account — Neon Sign

On examining the Pass Book received from you yesterday, we observe that you have debited our above account with US $2,000 on 4-3-19____. Our cheque book does not show any such withdrawal. Will you please check the matter immediately and rectify the mistake under advice to us. We are sending through bearer the Pass Book for necessary correction.

Thank you.

Yours faithfully,
For Central Industries Pvt. ltd.,
Sd/-
Director

Reply to the Above

Grams:
Tel:

THE COMMERCIAL BANK
Kuala Lumpur

Date: 13-3-19____

Ref. Comp/84

Messrs Central Industries Ltd.,
Hong Kong

Dear Sirs,

We thank you for your letter No. 16, dated 11th March, 19____.

We are sorry to note that through an oversight the amount of US $2,000 was debited to your account. The amount was actually to be debited to CONTROL SIGNS—almost a similar name. We have now made the necessary corrections in our accounts as also in your Pass Book and the same has been despatched under separate registered cover.

We regret very much for the inconvenience caused and assure you of our best service always.

Yours faithfully,
Sd/-
Manager

Reminder to the Bank Regarding Payment of Documents

Grams: Engineers
Tel: 268321

Registered
THOMSON ENGINEERS
Hornby Road
California

Date: 12th Jan., 19____

Ref. No: 1673

The Manager,
City Bank,
Valley Road,
Kentucky.

Sub: — Documents for US $400.00 in the name of Messrs. Topan & Sons.

Dear Sir,

1. The above documents were sent to you under registered cover vide our letter No. 1411 dated 9th Dec., 19____, which a request to deliver the same to the party concerned against full payment of the documents.

2. It was clearly mentioned in red ink in the last paragraph of the above letter the documents, if uncleared up to 24th Dec., 19____, may please be returned to us without seeking any further instructions.

3. As the documents have not been returned to us so far, we presume that the same have been released by the party. We, therefore, request you to please favour us with a bank draft for US $400 per return. On the other hand, if by any chance the documents are still pending, please return the same immediately.

Thank you.

Yours faithfully,
For Thomson Engineers,
Sd/-
Partner.

Legal Threat to the Bank Regarding Non-Payment of Documents

REGISTERED A.D.

Grams: Engineers
Tel: 286321

THOMSON ENGINEERS
Hornby Road
California

3rd Feb., 19____

Ref. No:—1871
The Manager,
City Bank,
Valley Road,
Kantucky.

Sub—Documents for US $400.00 in the name of Messrs Jones & Sons.

Dear Sir,

1. The above documents were sent to you under registered cover on the 9th Dec., 19____.

2. It was clearly marked on the covering letter that in case the documents are not returned by the part up to 24th Dec., 19____, the same may be returned without seeking any further instructions from us.

3. Having failed to receive any reply from you until 12th Jan., 19____, we sent you yet another registered letter bearing No. 1673 on the same date and requested you either to send us a draft or the documents per return.

4. We regret very much to say that until today we have heard nothing in the matter and we have every reason to believe that the payment of the documents has been received by you and the same is being delayed at your end deliberately.

5. We are now left with no choice except to insist payment of our documents within seven days from the date of this letter failing which we shall be obliged to pass on the matter to our legal advisers at your risk and cost. If by any chance, the documents are returned to us now, they will be refused equally at your risk and cost as this is contrary to our repeated instructions.

Thank you.

Yours faithfully,
For Thomson Engineers,
Sd/-
Partner.

Reply to the Above

CITY BANK
Valley Road
Kentucky.

Dated 16th Feb., 19____

Ref. No. — 131/73-74

Messers Thomson Engineers,
Hornby Road,
California.

Sub — Documents for US $400.00 in the name of Messrs Jones & Sons.

Dear Sir,

We thank you for your letter No. 1871 dated 3rd Feb., 19____.

The payment of the above documents has already been remitted to you by our draft No. A-13876, dated 3rd January, 19____, for US $400. Please, therefore, check up the matter at your end and inform us accordingly.

Thank you.

Yours faithfully,
Sd/-
Manager.

Non-Receipt of a Draft

Grams: Engineers
Tel.: 263821

THOMSON ENGINEERS
Hornby Road,
California

Dated: 8th Feb., 19____

Ref. No: 1899

The Manager,
City Bank,
Valley Road,
Kentucky.

Dear Sir,

We thank you for your letter No. 131/74 dated 6th Feb., 19____.

We have carefully checked our records and have not been able to trace the draft. It appears that you sent the same through an ordinary post and the same got misplaced somewhere in transit.

We, therefore, request you to please issue us a fresh draft.

Thank you.

Yours faithfully,
For Thomson Engineers
Sd/-
Partner

Letter to a Bank Enclosing Cheque for a Third Party

MOHAMMAD BROS.
The Mall
Lahore

16th April, 19____

The Manager,
Habib Bank Limited,
The Mall,
Lahore (Pakistan).

Dear Sir,

We enclose cheque No. .... dated .... for US $....... which please credit to the account of Messrs Tubewell Company Limited.

Please acknowledge the receipt of this letter.

Thank you.

Yours faithfully
For Mohamed Bros,
Sd/-
Partner.

Reply to the Above

HABIB BANK LIMITED
The Mall
Lahore

Date: 22nd April, 19____

Messrs Mohammad Bros.,
The Mall,
Lahore.

Dear Sirs,

With reference to your letter of 16th April, we have credited a sum of US$....... to the account of M/s. Tubewell Company Limited and have informed them accordingly.

Assuring you of our best co-operation always.

Yours faithfully,
Sd/-
Manager.

Letter Requesting the Bank to Issue a Sterling Draft

A.M.P. & COMPANY
Brass Baha Road,
Singapore.

Date: 19th Nov., 19____

The Manager,
State Bank of Singapore,
Singapore.

Dear Sir,

This is to request you to please supply us a Sterling Draft for 2,020 pounds, in favour of M/s. John Samuel & Co., London, debit the equivalent amount in our currency to our account.

Thank you.

Yours faithfully,
For A.M.P. & Company,
Sd/-
Director.

Reply to the Above

STATE BANK OF SINGAPORE
Singapore

23rd Nov., 19____

Messrs A.M.P. & Company,
Brass Baha Road,
Singapore.

Dear Sirs,

With reference to your letter dated 19th Nov., 19____ we enclose the Sterling Draft for 2,020 pounds.

We have debited your account with strati $ 4040 ($2 per pound plus $30 as draft charges).

Kindly acknowledge receipt.

Yours faithfully,
Sd/-
Manager

Requesting a Bank to Discount Bill

REGISTERED
UAE STEEL COMPANY
Elarab Square
Dubai

Date: 18th Jan., 19____

Ref: 973

The Manager,
Grindleys Bank Ltd.

Dear Sir,

Please discount of the following bills and place their amount to our credit.

Particulars of Bills	Amount
1...............	
2...............	
3...............	
4...............	
5...............	

Yours faithfully,
For UAE Steel Company
Sd/-
Partner.

Encls:— As Above.

Reply to the Above

GRINDLEYS BANK LTD.
Dubai.

Ref:—DB/13

Messrs UAE Steel Company,
Dubai.

Dear Sirs,

With reference to your letter No. 973 dated 18th January 19____ we have pleasure in informing you that a sum of US$ .... (after deducting our commission) has been credited to your account.

Yours faithfully,
Sd/-
Accountant/Manager.

Letter to a Bank Regarding Dishonoured Cheque

TORRID INDUSTRIES LTD.
Industry Road
Manchester

Date: 10th Dec., 19____

Ref. No. S/209

The Manager,
Lloyds Bank,
Manchester.

Dear Sir,

We are much surprised to find that our cheque No. N 16173 dated 1st Dec., 19____, for £1000 issued in favour of Brisk Industries has been dishonoured by you.

On checking our accounts, we find that there was a credit balance of Rs. 764 on 16th Nov. and a further sum of £600 was deposited with you on 27th Nov., vide cheque No. T 13472 dated 25th Nov. issued by Messrs Jason Bros. in our favour.

As you had enough time in collecting the proceeds of the cheque for £ 600, there is no reason why balance to our credit should have fallen short of honouring our cheque.

May we request you to please intimate us per return the reasons for dishonouring our cheque?

Yours faithfully,
For Torrid Industries Ltd.
Sd/-
Director.

Reply to the Above

LLOYDS BANK
Elgin Road
Manchester

Date: 13th Dec., 19____

Ref: No. DH/16

Torrid Industries Ltd.
Industry Road,
Manchester.

Dear Sirs,

We thank you for your letter No. S/209 dated 10th Dec., 19____ .

It appears to us that while depositing your cheque for £600 you forgot to note that it was a postdated cheque (it is dated 24th Dec., 19____) the proceeds of which could not be credited to your account and in the absence of any previous arrangement with us regarding overdraft facilities, we had no choice except to refuse payment of your cheque for £1,000.

We hope you will appreciate our being justified in our action. On the other hand, we would suggest that you may arrange with us a standing overdraft to meet any such eventuality in future.

Thank you.

Yours faithfully,
Sd/-
Manager.

Bank Informing his Client that his Current Account has been Overdrawn

NATIONAL AND GRINDLAYS BANK LTD.
Chamber Street
London

Dated: 12th May, 19____

Messrs Mitchel Bros.,
Chamber Street,
London.

Dear Sirs,

After encashing your cheque No. .... dated ..... for ...... issued in favour of Messrs ...... your account has been over-drawn by £ ...... We, therefore, request you to please remit us this amount at your earliest possible convenience as our Current Account Rules do not permit any such overdrafts without previous arrangement with the bank.

Thank you.

Yours faithfully,
Sd/-
Manager.

Letter to the Bank for a Certificate Required for Tax purposes

The Agent
Bank of Tokyo,
London.

Dear Sir,

I have deposited with you securities worth £200,000 as per details given below:

....

....

....

....

The interest and dividends on these Securities are being collected by you and credited to my Account.

As I require particulars of tax already deducted and interest collected on these Securities, I request you to please issue a certificate in my favour.

Thank you.

Yours faithfully,
Michael George,
492, Herring Street,
London.

Applying for Loan

OVERSEAS TRADERS
421 Central City Road
Leverpool

Date: 8th Sept., 19____

The Manager,
City Bank Limited,
Liverpool.

Dear Sir,

We are interested in getting a loan of £40,000 against our business property worth £200,000.

We shall be glad to have your terms at your earliest. The loan is required for a period of three years.

Thank you.

Yours faithfully,
Sd/-
For Overseas Traders.

Reply to the Above

CITY BANK LIMITED
Liverpool.

12th Sept., 19____

Messrs Overseas Traders
421, Central City Road,
Liverpool.

Dear Sirs,

We thank you for your letter dated 12th Sept., 19____.

We shall be glad to give you a loan of £40,000 against your property at 8% per annum.

We enclose herewith the necessary forms regarding mortgage of property.

Thank you.

Yours faithfully,
Sd/-
Manager.

Encls: As above

Another Reply (Negative)

M/s. Overseas Traders,
421, Central City Road,
Liverpool.

Dear Sirs,

We thank you for your letter dated 12th Sept., 19____.

We regret that we are unable to advance any loan against property, as of late this practice has been stopped by the banks.

Thank you.

Yours faithfully,
Sd/-
Manager.

Letter to a Bank regarding a Joint Account

PATTERSON & COMPANY
Kankas City

11th May, 19____.

The Manager,
Grindleys Limited,
Kankas City.

Sub:— Current Account—Patterson & Company.

Dear Sir,

At present, the above account is being operated by all the three partners of the firm jointly. In future, we wish to operate the same individually. We, therefore, request you to please send the necessary forms for signatures per return of post.

Thank you.

Yours faithfully,
Sd/-
For Patterson & Company,

Form of a Demand Promissory Note (Pro-Note)

18th April, 19____

£2,000.

On demand please pay to Messrs Alkinson & Bros. or order the sum of £2,000 being the cost of two packets sent through Bank of London, together with all charges for value received.

Sd/-
For Manager.

To,
Messrs Thomson & Co.,
T.T. Road,
London.

Form of a Sight (Pro-Note)

24th Oct., 19____

US $400.

Thirty days after sight, please pay to the order of the Bank of Manchester a sum of US $400 (Dollar Four Hundred only) for the value of goods received vide R/R No. 123456 dated 23-10-19____, as per details of goods on Bill No. 84 dated 23-10-19____.

For New Light Publishers,
Sd/-
Partner.

To,
M/s. Giverson Sons,
Book-sellers,
Florida.

Asking a Bank to Issue a Guarantee for Goods to be Cleared before Receiving Documents

CAPITAL INDUSTRIES LTD.
Broadway
New York

18th Feb., 19____

Ref. DIN/69

The Manager,
Bank of America,
Broadway,
New York.

Dear Sir,

We have been informed by our clearing agents that 17 cases addressed to us have arrived from Singapore per S.S. "VICTORY". While the Bill of lading and other documents have not yet been received, the goods are urgently required as they form the raw material of our product. May be, therefore, request you to please issue us your Bank's Guarantee so that we may present the same to the Customs and get the goods released. As soon as we receive the documents, we shall release your Guarantee from the Customs and return the same to you. In the meanwhile you may debit to our account the amount necessary as deposit.

Yours faithfully,
For Capital Industries
Sd/-
Director

Letter of Credit

NEW PRINTING WORKS
Bristol.

18th March, 19____

To,

The Manager,
Bank of America,
London.

Dear Sir,

This letter will be presented to you by our Sales Manager, Mr. John

Trevor, and we shall be obliged if you will honour his drafts up to £10,000 and debit to our account.

Yours faithfully,
Sd/-
For New Printing Works

Instructing a Bank to Honour Signature

YUSUFF BROS. (P) LTD.

Dated: 6th Jan., 19____

The Manager,
The Bank of Tokyo,
Tokyo.

Dear Sir,

Please note that from this date all cheques drawn on our Accounts will be signed by three Directors as heretofore and countersigned by Mr. L.M. Yusuff instead of Mr. N.T. Mohammad. Similarly, all cheques payable to us will be endorsed by Mr. Yusuff instead of Mr. Mohammad.

Yours faithfully,

Sd/-

For Yusuff Bros. Pvt. Ltd.

Letter to a Bank seeking Attestation of Signatures

NEW PRINTING WORKS
Bristol

14th Nov., 19____

The Agent,
Bank of America,
London.

Dear Sir,

As we wish to open another bank account with City Bank Ltd., so, we request you to please attest the below mentioned signature of all the partners of the above firm.

Thank you.

Yours faithfully,
Sd/-
For New Printing Works

Letter to a Bank Enquiring about Status of a Customer

BRITISH BANK
Harrington Street
London
(Private & Confidential)

28th August, 19____

The Manager,
The English National Bank,
George's Avenue,
London.

Dear Sir,

May we please request you to favour us with your opinion as to the means to and standing of the party whose name appears below. Please rest assured that any information you may favour us with, will be treated as strictly private and confidential.

Thanking you.

Name: Martin Jason
Designation: Partner.
Address: British Trading Co.,
Abbey Road,
London.

Yours faithfully,
Sd/-
Manager.

Reply to the Above

ENGLISH NATIONAL BANK
George's Avenue
London
(Private & Confidential)

Date: 31st Aug., 19____

The Manager,
The British Bank,
Harrington Street,
London.

Dear Sir,

With reference to your letter dated 28th Aug., 19____, we are enclosing the report as desired. Please note that the report is being sent in strictest confidence and the bank will not accept any responsibility whatsoever. Further, the name of this bank must not be disclosed in the event of passing on this report to anyone else.

Thank you.

Yours faithfully,
Manager.

Letter to a Bank for despatch of Documents of a Foreign Client

BASHEER TRADING CO.,
Sadar Bazar
Dubai

The Manager,
The Bank of UAE,
Monsur Road,
Dubai.

Dear Sir,

We are enclosing herewith four copies of our Foreign Bill No. 111 dated 23rd October, 19____, for US $1,200.

Two packets against the above bill have been sent to the party's Bankers and the details of each packet are also enclosed.

We are further enclosing Exchange Control Form No. 607803 in duplicate.

The documents may please be sent to the party's bankers, M/s. United Commercial Bank, Singapore, for payment after 30 days from the date of acceptance of the documents.

A net amount of US $1,200 is to be credited to our account on realisation and all bank charges to be collected from the party concerned.

Thank you,

Yours faithfully,
Sd/-
For Basheer Trading Co.

Form of Exchange to be submitted with the Foreign Documents

No........................ Date ....

Exchange for US $1,200.

Exchange (Second of the same tenor and dated being unpaid) to the order of Bank of UAE the sum of US $1,200 (Dollar One thousand two hundred only) for value received and exchange the same to the account of M/s. Roberston Ltd., E.L. Road, Singapore,

For Basheer Trading Co.,
Sd/-

To,

M/s Roberston Ltd.,
E.L. Road,
Singapore.

Bank Informing Position of Foreign Documents

BANK OF UK
Foreign Exchange Division
Fleming Street
London

Place ....
Date ....

Dear Sirs,

Our...................... No.......................... for......................

Drawn on...................

Yours Ref. ....

With reference to the above bill, we have to report as follows:

It has been paid........

It has been accepted by the drawees to mature on .... If remains unpaid for the following reason/s

Please instruct

Please arrange for payment/repayment immediately.

Yours faithfully,
Sd/- Manager.

Depositing a Dividend Warrant

A.S. GODWIN
31/1, Park Street,
London (UK)

4th May, 19____

Ref. No. 15/67

The Manager,
New Bank of UK,
L-Block,
Pont Street,
London.

Dear Sir,

I am sending herewith Dividend Warrant No. 52 for £7.80 received from Metal Distributors Limited, London.

Please credit the amount to the Savings Account of the undersigned No. 3650.

Thank you.

Yours faithfully,
Sd/-
(A.S. Godwin)

Returning Dividend Warrant/Cheque

NEW BANK OF UK
Park Street
London

Date 29th May, 19____

Ref. No.

Dear Sir,

We beg to advise that as your enclosed cheque for £ .... on .... has been received back unrealised for reason(s) given on the Memo attached thereto which please find enclosed, ... your account has been debited with £ .... plus .... on account of interest and postage.

Please acknowledge receipt and oblige.

Yours faithfully,
Sd/-
Manager.

Encl. As Above

Memo Showing Reason of Returning the Dividend Warrant

BANK OF AMERICA

New York

Date ....

Cheque No. .... for US $........ returned unpaid for reason No. ....

1. Payee's endorsement required. (la) Shareholder's discharge required in the place provided for. (1b) Please certify that the amount of this cheque is credited to payee's account only.

2. Payee's endorsement irregular; will pay on Bank's confirmation.

3. Payee's endorsement requires Bank's confirmation. (3a) Shareholder's discharge irregular.

4. Payee's endorsement irregular. Prefix 'For' for 'For' and on behalf of or 'Per pro'.

5. Payee's vernacular endorsement must be attested by a J.P. or Magistrate under official seal.

6. Translation of vernacular writing requires Bank's guarantee. (6a) Guarantee translation of vernacular writing required. (6b) Collecting Bank's confirmation requires clearing Bank's guarantee. (6c) Collecting Bank's discharge required in your favour.

7. Post-dated. (7a) Our of date. (7b) Date doubtful. (7c) Date irregularly written. (7d) Date incomplete. (7e) Cheque without date. (7f) Dividend warrant of date, please refer to the company. (7g) Cheque mutilated, requires Bank' guarantee.

8. Amount in words and figures differs.

9. .... requires Drawer's full signature.

10. Drawer's signature differs from the specimen accord with us.

11. Drawer's vernacular signature must be attested by your bank's Official.

12. Drawer's signature incomplete (12a) Drawer's signature required (12b) Title of the account required. (12c) Cheque irregularly drawn.

13. Crossed cheque must be presented through a Bank. (13a) This attached cheque will be received by us for collection. (13b) This attached draft is marked "Payee's account only".

14. Effects not cleared, please present again ......

15. Effects drawn against returned unpaid.

16. Not provided for. (16a) Not arranged for. (16b) Exceeds arrangements.

17. No advice, present again........

18. Full cover not received. (18a) Funds expected, please present again ....

19. Refer to Drawer. (19a) Insufficient funds. (19b) Account closed.

20. Payment stopped by the drawer. (20a) Cheque number differ. (20b) Cheque crossed to two Banks. (20c) Please present this cheque at the counter for encashment. (20d). Stamp required to be cancelled under authenticated initials.

21. Today's Clearing House stamp required. (21a) Receipt stamp required.

22. Cheque payable to a firm cannot be credited to your account unless specifically endorsed by the firm in your favour.

23. ....

Yours faithfully,
Sd/-
Acctt./Agent

Telegraphic Transfer

S.K. TOYS COMPANY
Esplanade
London.

Date: 4th Jan., 19____

The Manager,
Orient Bank,
Connaught Line,
London.

Dear Sir,

Kindly telegraphically transfer US $2500 from our current account to your branch in Broad Street, Singapore for credit to our account there.

Thank you.

Yours faithfully,
Sd/-
For S.K. Toys Company.

21
Insurance Correspondence

A. LIFE INSURANCE

Informing the L.I.C. Regarding Interest in Insurance

Date: 18th Sept., 19____

The Manager,
Life Insurance Corporation of UK,
London.

Sir,

I am interested in getting insured every member of my family.

Please send your agent to complete all the necessary formalities pertinent thereto.

Thank you.

Yours faithfully,
Albert Pinto
211, Hamilton Road,
London.

Reply to the Above

LIFE INSURANCE CORPORATION OF UK
London

Date: 21st Sept. 19____

Dear Sir,

We thank you for your letter dated 18th September, 19____.

We have today advised Mr. Jerry Alkins our insurance agent, to call on you on the morning of 26th September, 19____, at 8.00 A.M., to complete the necessary formalities.

He will also bring a medical practitioner for medical examination.

Yours faithfully,
Sd/-
Manager
Life Insurance Corporation of UK

Mr. Albert Pinto,
211, Hamilton Road,
London.

Medical Opinion Regarding the Family Members

LIFE INSURANCE CORPORATION OF UK

Date: 3rd Oct., 19____

Dear Sir,

The medical report of all the members is satisfactory except that of your younger brother who has not been found fit for the purpose of insurance.

Please send a cheque for £2,000 as the premium of insurance as per details furnished hereunder :-

1. Mr. Albert Pinto £600.00
2. Mr. Robert Pinto £400.00
3. Mr. Charles Pinto £200.00
4. Mrs. Agnes Pinto £800.00

Yours faithfully,
Sd/-
Manager
Life Insurance Corporation of UK

Mr. Albert Pinto,
211, Hamilton Road,
London.

Reply to the Above

Date: 7h Oct., 19____

Sir,

With reference to your letter dated 3rd October, I am enclosing herewith a Cheque No. KB 73814 dated 6th Oct. for £2,000.

Please acknowledge receipt and issue the necessary Policies.

Yours faithfully,
Sd/-
Albert Pinto

The Manager,
Life Insurance Corporation of UK,
London.

L.I.C. Asking for the Proof of Age

BRITISH LIFE INSURANCE CORPORATION
Grant Street
London

Date: 17th March, 19____

Mr. John Beverly,
12B, Rupert Road,
London.

Sub: Proposal for Life Insurance — £20,000.

Dear Sir,

We thank you for your letter enclosing Insurance Proposal as mentioned above.

In this regard, we wish to inform you that as per the latest rules of the corporation, you have to submit a documentary evidence in support of your age. We shall, therefore, appreciate your doing the same per return of post.

Yours faithfully,

Sd/-
Manager
B.L.I.C
London

Sending the Proof of Age

REGISTERED
12B, Rupert Road,
London

Date: 23rd May, 19____

The Manager,
British Life Insurance Corporation
Grant Street,
London.

Sub:— Proposal for Life Insurance — £20,000.

Dear Sir,

With reference to your letter dated 14th May, 19____, I am enclosing herewith Original Certificate of School Leaving Examination for your verification regarding my age.

Please return the Certificate at your earliest.

Thank you.

Yours faithfully,
Sd/-
John Beverly

Another Reply

12B, Rupert Road,
London.

Date: 19th March, 19____

The Manager,
British Life Insurance Corpn.,
Grant Street,
London.

Dear Sir,

I am in receipt of your letter dated 17th March, 19____.

I am surprised to find that you have asked me to submit a documentary evidence in support of my age. My age has already been admitted vide Policies Nos. 1384762 and 1892341 and I had mentioned this fact in the current proposal form also. Please, therefore, check up your records once again.

Yours faithfully,
Sd/-
John Beverly

L.I.C. Reminding about Proposal Form

L.I.C. OF U.K.
London

24th March, 19____

Mr. John Beverly,
12B Rupert Road,
London.

Dear Sir,

You will remember that it is almost two months when our agent. Mr. William Jones, called on you in response to your intention of taking a Life Insurance Policy, but we have not heard anything further from you since then. May we remind you that since 31st March is fast approaching, it is financially in your own interest to get a policy before that date, as you would be able to get a rebate in your income-tax. One the other hand if you need any further clarification of any point, please ring up the undersigned on 2873621 and the needful will be done immediately.

Yours faithfully,
Sd/-
B.L.I.C.
London

Reply to the Above

128 Robert Road,
London

Date : ....

The Manager,
B.L.I.C.
London.

Sir,

I thank you for your letter. As I had been out of London for the last five weeks, I could not look into the matter. I am now enclosing a proposal form duly filled for an insurance of £20,000. I hope you will find the same in order.

Yours faithfully,
Sd/-
John Beverly

B.L.I.C. Intimating about Dishonour of a Cheque

BRITISH LIFE INSURANCE CORPORATION
(Branch Unit No. 118)
Albert Avenue
London

Date: ....

Mr. Gregory Atkins,

Community Hospital,

Haley Road,

London.

Proposal: 113526

Dear Sir,

Your Cheque No. 56453 for £570.00 on the Bank of Tokyo, in payment of advance premium under the above proposal has been returned to us unpaid by our Bankers for the reason: "REFER TO DRAWER".

Our Premium-Deposit BOC 83276, dated 8-11-19____ issued to you, therefore, stands cancelled. We shall thank you to send us immediately a fresh remittance a fresh remittance of £570.00 in lieu of the dishonoured cheque. In the meantime the dishonoured cheque is retained by us pending fresh payment or return of Receipt Deposit Memorandum issued to you

Thank you.

Yours faithfully,
Sd/-
Branch Manager.

Returning of Cheque (Another Letter)

BRITISH LIFE INSURANCE CORPORATION
Centralised Cash Collection Centre,
Albert Avenue,
London.
Registered

Dated : ....

Mr. Tom Lewis,
15, Harpick Street,
London 3129.

Ref: Policy No. 6000398

Dear Sir/Madam,

We are returning herewith your cheque/Pay-Order No. 15405 dated 21-11-19____ for £186.56 drawn on the New Bank of London, for reason No. 12* detailed below:—

1. Policy number is not given.

2. Policy number seems to be wrong.

3. The name of the Unit to which the policy pertains has not been given.

4. The amount in words and figures differs.

5. The cheque has not been signed by the drawer.

The cheque pertains to .... separate Units and therefore .... separate cheques should be sent.

7. The cheque is mutilated.

8. The correction in date has not been signed by the drawer.

9. We do not accept third-party cheques.

10. The cheque is post-dated and as such is not acceptable.

11. A letter of Authority is required from the Drawer of the cheque, if he himself is not the Policy holder.

*12 Cheque is stale. Date be altered.

Please do the needful as pointed out above and send the cheque to us to enable us to adjust the amount properly.

An early compliance is requested.

Yours faithfully,
Sd/-
Office Incharge.

Encl: As above.

Provisional Receipt of Money (Before Acceptance of Proposal)

No. 183267

BRITISH LIFE INSURANCE CORPORATION

Northern Zone .... Divisional Officer

Full Name ....

Address ....

.... Branch

.............19____

Dear Sir/Madam,

We are advising our Divisional Office that the sum of £ .... has been received from you as a deposit, in payment of .... due .... under proposal/Policy No. .... on the life of .... If the payment is accepted, the Corporation's Official Receipt will be issued in due course, but in the meantime the amount has been kept in deposit involving no risk to the Corporation.

Reason for holding the amount in deposit:

1. Initial deposit towards a fresh proposal.
2. First Premium Receipt awaited from the Divisional Office.
3. Discounted value of a premium deposit.
4. Immediate payment of £ being interest for late payment ....
5. Immediately payment of balance of £ .... as the payment is short by this amount.
6. Receipt of revival instructions from Divisional Office as the payment of premiums under the policy has been discontinued.
7. Policy/Proposal does not pertain to this Branch Office.
8. ....

£ .... By Cash/Cheque/MO/Collecting Bank/Adjustment.

Yours faithfully,
Sr. Divisional/Branch Manager.
B.O.C. No.

Cashier

Notes: 1. If no official receipt or communication is received within 30 days, please write to the Divisional Office quoting the name of Branch, the Policy and Deposit Memorandum Numbers with the amount and the date of payment.

2. Please furnish us Policy or Proposal Number and name of previous Insurance Company, if any.

3. Please note to make payment of premiums to the office servicing your Policy in order to avoid delay in the issue of premium.

Acceptance of a Proposal

BRITISH LIFE INSURANCE CORPORATION
London

18th Oct., 19___

Mr. Denis Price,
Store Officer,
British Airways,
15, Chruch Road,
London.

<table>
<tr><td colspan="2">Sum Proposed</td><td colspan="2">Branch</td><td colspan="2">Unit 30</td></tr>
<tr><td colspan="2">£7,500/- (Pound Seven thousand and five hundred only)</td><td colspan="2">Inspector's Name,
Agent's name
Code Numbers</td><td colspan="2">Mr. Johnny Nesh
Mr. Jack Richardson</td></tr>
<tr><td>Proposal No. & Date</td><td>Plan and Term of Assurance</td><td>Name of the Life to be Assured</td><td>Age</td><td>Instalment Premium & Mode</td><td>Deposit, if any</td></tr>
<tr><td>110113
27.9-</td><td>11-33</td><td>Mr. Denis Price</td><td>28</td><td>£300</td><td>£
12-00
(113/107)</td></tr>
<tr><td>Decision of the Corporation</td><td colspan="4">s proposed at ordinary rate.</td><td>Balance to be paid £380.00</td></tr>
</table>

Dear Sir/Madam,

Your proposal for Assurance has been accepted by the Corporation on terms mentioned herein above and a Policy will be issued to you on payment of the amount of the First Premium as stated above, to the Corporation.

The amount of the First Premium should be paid immediately, as until it is paid, the Assurance is not in force and the Corporation retains the right to cancel the acceptance. If payment is not made within 30 days from the date of issue of this acceptance, evidence of continued good health may have to be produce at your expense.

It is most important to note that if any change in your occupation or any adverse circumstance connected with your financial position or the general health of yourself or that of your family, however unimportant you may consider the same, occurs between the date of proposal and the date of payment of the First Premium in full or the date of this issue of this acceptance, whichever is late, or if a proposal for assurance or an application for revival of a policy on your life, made to any office of the Corporation, has since the date of this proposal been withdrawn or dropped or declined or accepted at an increased premium or subject to a lien or on terms otherwise than as proposed or if you have been selected for service in any of the Branches of Military, Naval or Air Force Services, the assurance will be invalid and all moneys which shall have been paid in respect thereof forfeited unless intimation of such event is made in writing to the Corporation and this acceptance of your proposal is reapproved by the Corporation.

Yours faithfully,
Sd/-
Divisional Manager

REQUIREMENTS/REMARKS

1. Subject to the proof of age satisfactory to the Corporation being furnished to the Corporation before the corporation goes on risk.
2. Subject to declaration of continued good health satisfactory to the Corporation being produced, if the premium is not paid before ....

3. As desired by the proposed, the risk cover under the Policy will commence on .... to give benefit of lower age to the proposer, provided interest at 4% on the premium (s) is paid in case the premium (s) is/are not paid before ....

4. As desired by the proposer, the risk cover under Policy will commence on ..... to give benefit of lower age to the proposer, provided the first premium with interest at 4% thereon from the date of commencement amounting to £ ...... is paid within 30 days.

5. The next instalment of premium falls due on ....

6. The Policy if any when issued will cover accident risk on male life only.

7. The Policy if and when issued will be exclusive of the Disability Benefit.

8. The first premium receipt will be issued on receipt of your consent to our terms of acceptance on the enclosed slip.

9. This acceptance is issued in substitution of and cancelling the previous one dated ....

First Premium Receipt

BRITISH LIFE INSURANCE CORPORATION

London.

Dated: 18th Oct., 19____

Mr. Denis Price,
Store Officer,
British Airways,
15 Church Road,
London.

FIRST PREMIUM RECEIPT

Received the above-noted amount being the First Premium on a Policy of assurance for the plan and the amount indicated herein above.

<table>
<tr><td colspan="2">Sum Assured</td><td>Branch</td><td colspan="2">Unit 3</td></tr>
<tr><td colspan="2">£7,500/- (Pound Seven thousand and five hundred only)</td><td>Inspector's Name, Agent's name Code Numbers</td><td colspan="2">Mr. Johnny Nesh
Mr. Jack Richardson</td></tr>
<tr><td>Proposal No. & Date</td><td>Plan and Term of Assurance</td><td>Name of the Life to be Assured</td><td>Age</td><td>Instalment Premium & Mode</td></tr>
<tr><td>110113
27.9-</td><td>11-33</td><td>Mr. Denis Price</td><td>22</td><td>£ 380.00
Yearly</td></tr>
<tr><td>Decision of the Corporation</td><td colspan="4">As proposed at ordinary rate.</td></tr>
</table>

The acceptance of this payment places the Corporation on the risk with effect from the date of this receipt and on the terms and conditions of the said Policy of assurance which will be issued on the above-said life provided the terms and conditions of the letter of acceptance have been complied with

The Policy will be forwarded as soon as prepared.

Date of Commencement of Policy 9-11-19____

Balance Held on Deposit — Nil.

The next premium falls due on 9-11-19____

Stamp,
Sd/-
Branch Manager

L.I.C. Informing about Due Date of the Premium

MORGAN LIFE INSURANCE CORPORATION

Boston

18th Oct., 19___

Mr. Abdul Aziz,
Ocean View Road,
Boston.

Sir,

Ref: Policy No 168765

This is to advise you that the yearly premium of US $1,000 on the above policy falls due on 3rd Nov., 19____. Please remit the amount within a period of one month.

Yours faithfully,
Manager,
Morgan Life Insurance Corporation
Boston.

Joint Insurance

Pen Yang,
Airport Road,
Florida.
Date: ....

The Manager,
Norton Insurance Company,
Florida.

Dear Sir,

As I wish to have a joint Insurance Policy in the name of Self and my wife, I request you to please send me the rates and the necessary forms for the same.

Yours faithfully,
Sd/-
Peng Yang

Reply to the Above

Date: ....

Mr. Peng Yang,
Airport Road,
Florida.

Sir,

We thank you for your letter dated ....

While we are enclosing the necessary forms and rates of joint insurance, we would suggest that you may given us an appointment so that we may send our agent along with the doctor to complete all the formalities at one instance.

Yours faithfully,
Sd/-
N.I.C.
Florida.

Asking for Insurance Policies

9th Feb., 19____

To,
The Manager,
Lloyds Insurance Corporation,
Texas.

Sir,

As you are aware, all formalities for insurance of four members of my family were completed on 7th October, and a premium of US $2,000 sent to you on the same date. I regret to say that although three months have since passed, I have not yet received the policies.

Will you please look into the matter and do the needful per return?

Thank you,

Yours faithfully,
Tanako Toshiba
85, Main Street,
Texas.

Letter of the L.I.C. Regarding Nomination or Assignment

Mohammad Amin,
160, Golf Course Road,
Houston Road.
16th May, 19____

The Manager,
New Insurance Corporation,
Houston.

Ref: Policy No. 168765

Sir,

The above policy stand in my personal name. As I have now got married, I wish to assign/nominate my policy to my wife.

Please let me know the necessary procedure and formalities to be observed.

Thank you.

Yours faithfully,
Sd/-
Mohammad Amin

Reply to the Above

Mr. Mohammad Amin
Golf Course Road,
Houston.

Ref: Policy No. 168765

Sir,

We acknowledge the receipt of your letter dated 16th May — regarding nomination/assignment of the above policy.

A copy of Assignment/Nomination Form is enclosed. Please fill in the same and return to us to enable us to register the Assignment/Nomination.

Yours faithfully,
Sd/-
Manager,
N.I.C.
Houston.

Requesting the L.I.C. for Paid-up Policy

Dated : ....

To,

The Manager,
Life Insurance Corporation of UK,
London.

Dear Sir,

I am the holder of the above policy of £25,000 and have paid premiums up-to-date. Unfortunately of late my business had gone down as I have suffered heavy losses in the same. I do not find any prospects of improving in the near furture and hence my inability in paying any more premiums. May I, therefore, request you to please convert the above policy into a paid up policy and let me know the amount that will be paid to me at the same time of maturity of the same?

Thank you.

Yours faithfully,
Sd/-
David Jackson
Down Street,
London.

Reply to the Above

LIC OF UK
London

Dated: ....

David Jackson
Down Street
London

Ref: Policy No. 7133381

Sir,

We are in receipt of your letter dated—regarding the above policy.

We are indeed sorry to learn that you have suffered heavy losses in your business and wish to convert the above policy into a Paid-up one.

In fact, this is the time when we can be of some assistance to you. If you desire, we can immediately advance you a loan of £...........at ____% per annum. This might help you in re-establishing your business. Please think over once again before you finally decide in having the policy paid-up.

As for the paid-up value of the policy, the same is £ ...... from 1st April, 19...........

Yours faithfully,
Sd/-
Manager
L.I.C. of UK
London

Applying for a Loan

128 Rupert Road,
London.

Dated : ....

The Manager,
B.L.I.C.
Albert Avenue
London.

Sub: Loan against Policy No. 1234567

Dear Sirs,

I am holder of the above policy and have paid premiums up-do-date.

I intend to draw a loan against my policy and would appreciate your informing me per return the necessary procedure for the same.

Thank you.

Yours faithfully,
Sd/-
John Beverly.

Reply to the Above

B.L.I.C.
London.

Dated: ....

Mr. John Beverly,
128 Rupert Road,
London.

Sub: Loan against Poliçy No. 1234567

Sir,

We thank you for your letter on the subject cited above.

As per rules of the Corporation, a maximum sum of £6,250 can be granted to you as loan on the above policy. The loan can be retained by you for any period you wish subject only to the maturity of the policy.

The loan will bear an interest of 6% per annum and a minium of 6 months interest is payable even if the amount is repaid earlier. Further, you will have to mortgage your policy and sign a loan-bond paper which will carry non-judical stamps worth £1.50.

Yours faithfully,
Manager,
B.L.I.C.
London.

B.L.I.C. Sending Loan Quotations

THE LIFE INSURANCE CORPORATION OF UK
London Divisional Office,
Policy Holders' Servicing Department,
Please address all your communications at the above address.

Date: 10-3-19____

Ref. PHS/Loan
Mr. David Mart,
1, West-End Street,
London.

Ref — Deptt., P.H.S.
LOAN QUOTATION
Policy NO. 6000398

Dear Sir,

With reference to your letter/application of 9-3-19 — we have to inform you that the desired/maximum loan of £1480 is available on security of the above Policy taking premium due 9-11-19 — as paid, on our usual terms of interest @ 6% per annum payable every half-year.

Our loans being certain for six months, no repayment can be accepted within that period unless six months interest is paid.

In the event of your requiring this sum, please forward to us the above Policy and a remittance of £..... for stamp duty on the Bond when we shall issue the necessary documents for completion by you and a sum of £ .... will be appropriated from the loan as under:

....

....

....

Yours faithfully,
Sd/-
Sr. Divisional Manager.

Specimen of a Loan Bond-Form

L.I.C. of UK
NORTHERN ZONE.
LOAN BOND

I/we, the Borrowers mentioned in the schedule hereof, having this day received from the life Insurance Corporation of UK (hereinafter referred to as the Corporation) an advance by way of loan of the sum as stated in the said schedule against the security of the policy described in the said schedule which has been deposited by me/us with the said Corporation DO HEREBY forself/selves and my/our respective heirs, executors and administrators covenant and agree with the said Corporation, their successors and assigns as follows:

1. That the said Policy shall be held by the said Corporation, this successors and assigns as security for the payment of the said advance and of interest thereon as hereinafter mentioned and of all expenses which may be incurred in connection therewith, and that without prejudice to the prior charge in favour of the said Corporation in respect of the advance already granted by the said Corporation on the security of the said Policy and still subsisting as mentioned in the Schedule which is hereby confirmed.

2. That the said advance shall not be repaid within a period of six months from the date on which the loan is settled.

3. To pay interest to the said Corporation, their successors and assigns at the office mentioned in the said schedule at the rate of 6 per cent year compounding half yearly on the said advance, the first payment of interest to be made on the date specified in the said schedule.

4. When called upon to make repayment at the said office of the said advance with all interest which may be due thereon on being given 3 months, notice to the effect.

5. That the Corporation, their successors and assigns shall not be bound to accept the repayment of the said advance unless tendered in full.

6. That in the event of failure to repay the said advance when required as aforesaid to pay interest in terms of these presents on the dates here in before mentioned or within a calendar month after each due date respectively the said Policy shall be held. Without the necessity of any notice being given, to be forfeited the said Corporation, their successors and assigns, and the Corporation shall be entitled to apply the Surrender Value allowable in respect of the said Policy in terms of their Regulations and Conditions in payment of the said advance, interest and expenses, the balance, if any, of such Surrender Value to be accounted for the party, entitled thereto.

7. That in case the Policy shall mature or become a claim by death, when the amount of the said advance or any portion thereof shall remain outstanding, the Corporation shall be entitled to deduct such amount together with all the interest upto the date of maturity or of death, as the case may be, form the policy money, and the balance only shall become due and payable under policy.

8. This document shall in all respects be deemed to have been made and completed at — (London).

And as security for the said advance interest and expenses DO HEREBY assign to the said Corporation, their successors and assign the said policy and the sum of the sums to become due under the same, either or surrender or otherwise.

DECLARATION

I/We hereby declare that I/We have not served on any office of the Life Insurance Corporation of UK any notice of assignment or reassignment in respect of the above policy expect those of any already registered by this Life Insurance Corporation of UK or the interest who issued the above Policy nor shall I/we serve on any office of the said Corporation any notice of assignment or reassignment before payment of the Loan Value, Surrender Value.

Signature of the Assured................

Signature of the Assignee (s)...........

Date............

Reminder for Loan

V.V. Richard,
51, West-End Street,
New Jersey.
Date: 6th June, 19.......................

Urgent

The Sr. Divisional Manager,
National Life Insurance Corporation,
New City Complex,
New Jersey.

Re. Policy No. 6000398 — Loan

Dear Sir,

It is noted with great regret that in spite of my sending a M.O. for US $...... for purchasing bond in connection with the grant of a loan of US $2000 against the above policy, I have not as yet received any intimation from you although it is now more than a month when the amount was remitted to you.

May I expect your cheque by return of post?

The above policy was sent to you on 13th April and I have already reminded you about the same.

Yours faithfully
Sd/-
V.V. Richard

Forwarding Insurance Policy for Loan Purpose

V.V. Richard
51, West-End Street,
New Jersey.
Date: 26-3-19 —

The Sr. Divisional Manager,
National Life Insurance Corporation
New City Complex
New Jersey.

Sub: Loan against Policy No. 60000398.

Dear Sir,

With reference to your letter No. PHS/Loan dated the 10th March, 19

—, on the subject cited above, I am forwarding herewith the above Policy. The amount of IS$ ___ towards stamp duty is begin remitted separately by Money Order. Please issue me the loan of US $2000 on your usual' terms at your earliest.

Yours faithfully,
Sd/-
V.V. Richard

L.I.C. Sending Bond for a Loan

LIFE INSURANCE CORPORATION OF USA
Northern Zone

Ref. Mis/10a

Steve Lewis
1, West End Street,
USA.

Sub : POLICY LOAN

Dear Policy Holder,

1. We are in receipt of your remittance towards the stamp fee on Loan Bond and accordingly a duly stamped Loan Bond is being sent to out for completion by the party or parties concerned as detail below.

2. On your returning the Loan Bond duly completed by the party or parties concerned and on your furnishing the requirements as stated in item IV of the schedule, we shall proceed further with the settlement of the loan by sending to you the balance after adjustment of dues by drawing a cheque on the Corporation's Bankers.

3. Full instructions for completion of the Loan Bond are given on the Loan Bond Form

4. Please read these instructions carefully and comply with the requirements in order to avoid our having to return the Loan Bond as incomplete or improperly completed.

SCHEDULE

Policy No.   Life Assured

I. Loan Bond for US $____ is sent herewith duly stamped.

II. Stamp fee US$_______recieved.

III. Loan Bond is required to be completed by

(1)

(2)

(3)

IV. While returning the Loan Bond after completion, Please send along therewith.

(1) Policy

(2) Assignment Deed ( )

(3) Declaration Slip re. non-existence of any assignments of the policy than those registered with the Corporation (From enclosed with previous letter).

(4) Authority letter. (Form enclosed)

V. When the Loan Bond and other documents are received duly completed, loan will be granted and after adjustment of dues as stated in the Corporation's letter dated _____________a cheque for the balance will be sent to you on ______________Bank Ltd. at____________

If you wish, the balance to be paid by money order or by Bank Draft at your cost, please write to us for the same.

Yours faithfully,

Sd/-

Sr. Divisional Manager

Note: In your reply please quote our Ref.....................

Returning a Loan Bond

REGISTERED

1, West-End Street,
USA
Date : 26th June, 19__

Sub Divisional Manager,
Divisional Office,
Life Insurance Corporation of USA,
Northern Zone,
USA.

Sub: Loan against Policy No. 6000398

Dear Sir,

This has references to your letter No. Misc/Loan dated 14.2.19... on the subject cited above. Loan Bond duly completed is returned herewith.

It is, however, noted with great regret that I am corresponding for this loan for the last 4 months but as yet I have not received the same. Will you please send me the cheque by return of post?

Please note that the above policy is with you and not with me and yet you are asking me to send the same to you along with this loan bond, vide Clause IV (1).

Yours faithfully,
Sd/-
Steve Lerwis

Remitting Amount of Loan

LIFE INSURANCE CORPORATION OF USA
New York Divisional Office

2, St. Church Lane,
New York.
Date: 9-7-19____

John Dair
12, Free Street,
New York.

Ref: Dept. H.P.S. Policy No......

Dear Sir,

We have received your letter dated _ ___ forwarding therewith the above Policy/Policies, the Deed of Assignment and the completed loan bond/s for US $____.

The completed loan bond/s being in order, we have ___settled the Loan transaction. After appropriating from the loan amount of US $______as detailed below, we send herewith by money order/our ______ crossed Cheque No. _____ for US $_____drawn in your favour on the ____ in payment of the balance loan amount.

PARTICULARS OF ADJUSTMENT

....

....

....

The official receipts in respect of item numbers.....................and Temporary Receipt Nos.............in respect of item numbers.......adjusted are enclosed. The official receipt for item number.............will be issued to you by our.............Office in due course.

Yours faithfully,
Sd/-
Sr. Divisional Manager

Repayment of Insurance Loan

Dated: 18th May, 19____

REGISTERED A.D.

The Manager,
Life Insurance Corporation of USA,
New York Divisional Office,
P.O. Box No. 688,
USA.

Dear Sir,

I am enclosing two Cheques for US $70 and US $1000 respectively bearing Nos...and dated 19th May, 19__________.

The amount of US $1000 is towards the loan advanced to me. Please return my Life Insurance Policy No. 6000398.

Thank you.

Yours faithfully,
Sd/-
John Dair,
12, Free Street,
New York.

B. LIFE INSURANCE AGENCY

Apply for an Agency

John. M. Samuel,
16, Williams Street,
USA.
Dated : 14-8-19____

To,

The Manager,
Life Insurance Corporation of USA,
New York.

Dear Sir,

I wish to take a 'Life Insurance Agency'. Please send me the necessary forms for the same.

Yours faithfully,
Sd/-
John M. Samuel.

Reply to the above

LIFE INSURANCE CORPORATION OF USA
New York

26th August, 19____

Mr. John M. Samuel,

With reference to your letter dated 14th August, 19___ , we are enclosing 'Insurance Agency Form'.

We have advised Mr. Alfred Robert our Development officer of that area to contact you and advise you further in the matter.

Yours faithfully,
Sd/-
Life Insurance Corporation of USA

Specimen of the Agency Application form

LIFE INSURANCE CORPORATION OF USA

Northern Zone

____________Division ________Branch

Abstract of the Agency Application Form

1. Name of the Agent ....
2. Date of Birth ....
3. Educational qualifications ....
4. Present occupation (with name & address of employer, if any) ....
5. Past business experience ....
6. Whether whole-time or part time ....
7. If related to any of the ....

Corporation's (a) Employees (b)

Agents or (c) Medical Examiners,

his name, designations and territory

where he works

Name ....
Designation ....
Centre ....
Code NO. ....

8. Date of Application

REFERENCES :-

1. Name	2. Name ....
Address	Address ....
Special remarks, if any	Special remarks, if any

DEVELOPMENT OFFICER

Name___________

Code No.___________

Special remarks, if any.___________

____

L.I.C. Information Regarding Receipt of an Application

LIFE INSURANCE CORPORATION OF USA
New York

New York Division,
118 Branch.
Date: 31-8-19

Mr. John M. Samuel,
16, Williams Street,
New York.

Re: Your Application for an Agency

Dear Sir,

We have received through our Development Officer your application for agency to canvass life insurance business for the Corporation for agency to canvass life insurance business for the Corporation along with an application for Licence duly completed by you and addressed to the controller of Insurance for the grant of a licence to work as an agent. We have also received US $50 sent by you towards the licence fee, and receipt No. 789 556 in respect thereof is enclosed herewith.

We have forwarded your application for licence to the Controller of Insurance and as soon as we receive the licence and, provided no adverse report in the meantime is received by us from any source, we shall issue the necessary Appointment Letter to you authorising you to work as an Agent of the Corporation. In the meanwhile, we are attaching you to our Development Officer, Shri Alfred Robert, so that he may give of the necessary training for conducting your agency and render you the necessary help in booking business, and we suggest that you may now get in touch with him so that he may start giving you the necessary training.

We also recommend our 'Manual for Agent' which you will find of considerable interest and assistance to you in your work as an agent. This is sold to our agents at a subsidised price or US $2.00 and on receipt of this amount from you, we shall send you a copy of the Manual.

Since your application for licence appears to be in order, we do not think there will be any difficulty for you to get the licence from the Controller of Insurance and on this presumption we shall have no objection to your canvassing life insurance business for the Corporation. While an Agency Code Number will be allotted to your proposed agency on receipt of the first proposal this, in no case, should be a date prior to the date of this letter. We would like to make it clear that if, for any reason, the issue of licence is delayed or declined, we will not be in a position to allow you credit of the business secured or completed before the actual commencement of the licence. Please note that the Code Number, when allotted, should be mentioned in your Agents Reports, correspondence, etc.

With best wishes for your success,

Yours faithfully,
Sd/-
Branch Manager

L.I.C. Sending Appointment Letter for Working as an Insurance Agent

Date: 7-9-19—-

Mr. John M. Samuel,
16, Williams Street,
New York.

Re. Issue of an Appointment Letter

Sir,

We have pleasure to enclose in triplicate your Appointment Letter as an agent. The original is meant for your record whereas the other two are to be returned to this office duly signed by you in token of your having accepted the terms and conditions contained therein.

Please acknowledge receipt and arrange to return two copies of the Appointment Letter at an early date, as otherwise the commission shall be with held by us.

Your Licence No. L — 53662 valid up to 14-9-11— is also enclosed.

Yours faithfully,
Sd/-
Branch Manager

Specimen of a Licence

Not Transferable

GOVERNMENT OF USA
OFFICE OF THE CONTROLLER OF INSURANCE
Licence No. L-53662
(See Rule 16-A of Insurance Rules 1939)
Licence to Act as an Agent Under Part II of the Insurance Act, 1938,

To be filled in by the Applicant in block letters	Mr. John M. Samuel 16, Williams Street New York

Having paid the prescribed fee and having made the necessary Declaration is hereby authorised to act as an Insurance Agent for three years from 14-9-19— Dated 13-9-19—

Signature of the Licence holder—-

Sd/-
Controller of Insurance

The licence is not valid unless it bears a facsimile of the signature of the Controller of Insurance and initials of a person authorised by him in this behalf and the signature of the licence holder. The latter should put his signature as soon as the licence is received.

Returning Copies of an Appointment Letter

14th Sept., 19-

The Branch Manager,
Life Insurance Corporation of USA,
New York,

Dear Sir,

I thank you for your letter dated 7th Sept.___

I am enclosing herewith two copies of appointment letter duly signed.

Thank you.

Yours faithfully,
Sd/-
John M. Samuel
16, Williams Street,
New York.

Writing for Commission

8th, Dec 19__R_

Sub: Policy No. 2422753

Dt. 15-9-19— in the name of Mr. David D'Souza

Sir,

With further reference to the subject cited above, I regret so say that have not yet received your cheque towards my commission.

I shall appreciate sending me the same per return.

Thank you.

Yours faithfully,
Sd/-
John M. Samuel,
16, Williams Street,
New York.

Reply to the Above

LIFE INSURANCE CORPORATION OF USA
New York

Dated : 16-12-19____

Ref: BO/dev/118.

Shri John M. Samuel,
AG. Code No. 29863-III
Re : Proposal No. 2422753

Dear Sir,

We have with held the 1st commission on the above mentioned proposal due to the following reasons:-

1. Age not admitted
2. Licence expired since....................
3. Agents of own life case.
4. Copy of Appointment Letter duly signed not-received.
5 ....

Please comply with the above requirement for our further action.

Yours faithfully,
Sd/-
Branch Manager.

c.c. to Sri —, D.O. Code No.—, for information and necessary action.

Sd/-
Branch Manager.

Submitting the Age-Proof

Date: 24-14-19——

The Manager,
L.I.C. of USA,
New York.

Dear Sir,

With reference to your letter No. BO/dev/118, dated 16th Dec., 19 — I am enclosing herewith the Matriculation Examination certificate of Mr. David D'Souza in support of his age.

Please do the needful per return.

Yours faithfully,
Sd/-
John M. Samuel,
16, Williams Street,
New York.

L.I.C. enclosing Cheque for Commission

LIFE INSURANCE CORPORATION OF USA
New York

Dated: 4th Jan, 19—-

Mr. John M. Samuel,
16, Williams Street,
New York.

Dear Sir,

With reference to your Letter dated 24th December, 19— we wish to advise you that the age of Mr. David D'Souza has been admitted. His Matriculation Examination Certificate is returned herewith.

A cheque for US$..............towards the commission on the first premium is also enclosed.

Yours Faithfully,
Sd/-
Manager

L.I.C. informing regarding Non-Completion of the required Business

LIFE INSURANCE CORPORATION OF USA
Branch Unit. No. 118,
New York

Dated : 25-3-19____

Ef: BO/dev/118
Mr. John M. Samuel,
16, Williams Street,
New York.

Re : Your Agency Code No. 2986311

Dear Sir,

You have completed a business of US $6000 on three lives with us against the requisite quota of business on six lives in your current Agency year. As such, in accordance with the provisions of the clause No. 2/4 of the Letter of Appointment issued to you, the Agency will come to an end with effect from 31-3-19— unless, you completed the requisite quota during the period from 1-4-19— to 30-3-19—-

You, are therefore, requested to make all possible efforts to complete the quota as stated above during this period, so that your Agency may be continued.

Further please note that no extension will be allowed to you. If you have already completed the business quota, please treat this letter as cancelled.

Wishing you all success,

Yours faithfully,
Sd/-
Branch Manager

Letter from the LIC to Agents and Development Officers Regarding Lapses

LIFE INSURANCE CORPORATION OF USA
Central Office, P.B. NO. 252
Florida 54389

A.B.C.
Chairman

Date: 3rd Jan., 19___

Rre: Lapses

Dear Friends,

Today I am addessing this Letter to you on an important aspect of the Corporation working, *viz.* 'Lapsation'. We have not been able to bring down the rate of lapsation to any significant extent. As you know, for the Corporation as a whole 12% of 15% of the new business slapses after payment of the first instalment of premium. Such business which lapses, hardly does any credit to any one. While 15% in the overall average, there are divisions with over 30% lapse-experience. Apart from wasteful efforts in putting such policies on the books, we have found that such business causes serious loss to the Corporation as the expenses incurred far exceeds the income received thereunder. Apart from this, there are losses on account of policies becoming paid up immediately after two years. All these losses will eat into the profit of the Corporation, affecting its ability to maintain bonuses, not to speak of increasing them.

I needs no argument to say that such lapses should be eliminated. A little care at the stage of cancassing of the business can go a great deal in reducing the extent of such lapses which occur immediately after payment of the first instalment of the premium. One has to conclude that these lapses arise primarily due to selling which does not take into account the genuine needs of the policy-holder.

I, therefore, request you to take adequate care at the time of canvassing the proposal and ensure that the proposal remains in the books of the Corporation. This will help in cutting out one of the sources of loss to the Corporation which is of prime importance, particularly in the current context of increasing costs of management.

I am planning to launch a special drive this year for clearance of deposits substantial reduction in our lapses, particularly lapses within the first policy year and revival of lapsed policies. I seek the active co-operation of all the members of our field force—Agents, Development Officers and Branch Officials—as well as of our administrative staff for the success of this drive.

Yours sincerely,
Sd/-
Chairman

To

All Agents and Development Officers.

Submitting a Claim

Date: 29-23-19—-

The Manager,
Life Insurance Corporation of USA,
Florida.

Sub: Policy No. 183721 — Mr. R. Fernandez

Dear Sir,

My client, Shri R. Fernandez expired of natural death on 11-3-19—

I am enclosing the necessary papers duly completed and would appreciate your sending a cheque for the amount to Mrs. Ann Fernandez

Yours faithfully,
Sd/-
Licence No. D 1603
Connaught Place,
Florida

Sending the Cheque

LIFE INSURANCE CORPRATION OF USA
Florida

Dated 13-4-19

Mrs. Fernandez
42, Statian Road,
Florida.

Sub : Policy No. 183721 - Mr. Fernandez

Dear Madam,

With reference to the subject referred to above, we are enclosing our cheuqe No..............dated............for towards the full settlement of your claim

Yours faithfully,
Sd/-
Life Insurance Corporation of USA
Florida

BUSINESS INSURANCE

Insurance of Goods Against All Risks

ISMAIL & BROS.
Penang

Date : 14th Jan., 19___

The Manager,
Confident Insurance Co.,
Penang.

Dear Sir,

Please insure the goods as per list attached in the name of Messrs. Khurshid Ahmed & Co. The goods are to be insured against all risks. Kindly Let us know the amount payable so that we may send the cheque.

Thank you.

Yours faithfully,
For Ismail & Bros.,
Sd/-
Manager
Penang

Reply to the Above

CONFIDENT INSURANCE CO.
Penang

Dated 17-1-19-

Messrs. Ismail & Bros.,
Penang.

Dear Sirs,

We thank you for your letter dated 14th Jan., 19 ____, sending a statement of goods to be insured.

The Insurance Policy is being prepared and will be sent to you within three/four days. In the meanwhile please send us a cheque for US $110 as premium as per advice enclosed. Your risk stands covered with effects from 21-1-19....

Yours faithfully,
Sd/-
Manager.

Insuring Goods lying in a Godown

ABDULLA INDUSTRIES
A. Manzur Street
Kuala Lumpur

The Manager,
Canada Insurance Co.,
Kuala Lumpur.

Dear Sir,

We are enclosing a statement of goods lying in our godown at the above. Please insure the same to their total value of US $5000 and let us know per return the amount of premium we have to pay.

Thank you.

Yours faithfully,
For Abdullah Industries,
Sd/-
Accountant/Manager

Encl: As above.

Reply to the Above

Reply to the above will be almost on the same lines as for the foregoing letter.

Asking for Insurance Advice

NEW TEXTILE MILLS
Bangkok

Dated: 10-4-19-

The Manager,
Capital Insurance Co.,
Bangkok.

Dear Sir,

We wish to send twenty consignments each worth US $2000 to Singapore, Jakarta Penang and some countries of the Middle East.

The goods will be sent first by Road Transport and then loaded in the steamer wherever abroad. They will be packed in accordance with the usual requirements

We shall appreciate your sending us an outline of the working of such a policy.

Thank you

Yours faithfully,
Sd/-
Manager

Reply to the Above

CAPITAL INSURANCE COMPANY

Bangkok

M/s. New Textile Mills,
Bangkok.

15th April, 19____

Dear Sirs,

We thank you for your letter dated 10th April, 19-

We have pleasure in informing you that we shall be only too glad to cover all risks of fire, theft, pilferage, etc.

The policy would carry an interest of 1.70%.

The original policy will be fowarded to you as soon as the declaration form, to be filled in and signed by you with each despatch, is received.

We hope the facilities offered will suit you and you will favour us with your definite proposal per return.

Thank you.

Yours faithfully,
Sd/-
Manager.
Capital Insurance Company

Loss by Fire

ALFA UTENSILS

Sri Lanka

The Manager,
The New Insurance Co.
Sri Lanka.

Re: Fire Policy No. 1117

Dear Sir,

We regret to inform you that a fire broke out in our godown located at the above address at about 10.00 p.m. last night. The fire was first noticed by Jaya Surya, the night watchman of the locality, who immediately contacted the fire brigade on phone.

The fire brigade reached there at 10.30 p.m. but by that time the premises had been completely gutted and it was only at 1.00 a.m. that the fire brigade was able to extinguish the fire successfully. The undersigned reached there at 11.00 p.m. on having been informed of the incident by the watchman on phone.

We estimate a total loss of US $1000 and request you to please send your Surveyor or Inspector to assess the loss and let us know what formalities are to be completed for putting up a claim for the loss.

Yours faithfully,
For Alfa Utensils,
Sd/-
Proprietor.

Reply to the Above

THE NEW INSURANCE CO.
Sri Lanka

20th Nov., 19—

M/s. Alfa Utensils
Sri Lanka.

Dear Sirs,

With reference to your letter dated 19th Nov., 19—, please be informed that our surveyor, Mr. D. B. Gandhi will can on you on 22nd Nov., 19— to assess the loss. Meanwhile please fill in the attached form and return the same by first mail.

Your faithfully,
Sd/-
Manager

Encl: As above

Letter Enclosing Cheque for Settlement

THE NEW INSURANCE CO.
Sri Lanka

10th Dec., 19

Messrs Alfa Utensils,
Sri Lanka.

Dear Sirs,

With further reference to your claim form and our surveyor's report we are sending herewith a cheque for US$ 800 in full and final settlement.

Please send us your official receipt for the amount.

Yours faithfully,
Manager

Encl: One cheque.

Asking for Travelling Insurance

18th March, 19—-

The Manager,
Sunlight Insurance Company,
Hong Kong.

Dear Sir,

I am leaving for Saigon for an on-the-spot study of situation now prevailing, on 26th March 19 - and would like to have a Travelling Insurance Policy to the tune of US $50,000.

Please send me the necessary forms for completion and let me know the total amount of premium to be paid. I shall be in Saigon for five days form 27th March 10 1st April, 19—

Thank you.

Yours faithfully,
Sd/-
George Mathews
14, M.G. Road,
Hong Kong.

Reply to the Above

SUNLIGHT INSURANCE COMPANY
Hong Kong

18th March, 19—-

Mr. George Mathews,
14, M.G. Road,
Hong Kong.

Dear Sir,

We thank you for your letter dated 16th March, 19-

We are enclosing proposal form to be filled in by you.

We need hardly mention that in view of Saigon being a 'troubled area' you should fill the details minutely and accurately.

Please return the forms together with a cheque or US $75 (premium) to cover the risks.

Yours faithfully.
Sd/-
Manager.
Encl: As above.

Request to Insure Goods Shipped—All Risks

DIWAN BROS.
College Street
Bangkok

13th Dec., 19—-

The Manager,
General Insurance Company,
Chowringhee Square,
Bangkok.

Dear Sir,

Please insure for us against all risks US $1000 value of five cases of books marked: NMS—5 and shipped for account of Messrs. Rangoon Traders, Rangoon, by "S.S. REGAL" sailing on 7th Jan., 19—-

Thank you.

Yours faithfully,
Sd/-
Partner

Complaint Regarding an Insurance Policy

DIWAN BROS.
College Street
Bangkok

16th Jan., 19____

The Manager,
General Insurance Company,
Chowringhee Square,
Bangkok.

Sub: Policy No. 1730

Dear Sir,

We have today received the above policy and on going through the contents of the same, we find that you have made no mention of "loss through pilferage". On the contrary, if you see the Proposal Form of the above Policy, you will find that this clause is specifically mentioned therein. We are, therefore, returning the policy herewith and shall appreciate your inserting the necessary words to cover loss through pilferage also.

Thank you.

Yours faithfully,
Sd/-
Partner

Complaint Regarding Damaged Goods

UNIVERSAL TRADERS
Regent Road
Singapore

4th Jan., 19____

The Manager,
Sunlight Insurance Company,
Hong Kong.

Dear Sir,

We are enclosing a copy of the report of the Customs Authorities regarding goods worth US $2000 which we received in damaged condition. These articles were included by our Singapore Agents in the Consignment which was sent by "S.S. VISCOUNT"

As the consignment was fully insured against all risks, we request you to please assess our loss and favour us with your cheuqe at an early date.

Thank you.

Yours faithfully,
For Universal Traders,
Sd/-
Partner

Reply to the Above

SUNLIGHT INSURANCE COMPANY
Hong Kong.

7th June., 19__

Messrs Universal Traders,
Regent Road,
Singapore.

Dear Sirs,

We thank you for your letter dated 4th January, 19 ___ and are sorry to learn about the loss you have suffered. We are arranging to have the damage assessed within this week.

Thank you.

Yours faithfully,
Sd/-
Manager.

Another Reply

SUNLIGHT INSURANCE COMPANY,
Hong Kong

Messrs Universal Traders,
Regent Road.
Singapore.

Dear Sirs,

We thank you for your letter dated 4th January, 19 ___ and are sorry to learn about the loss you have suffered.

We suggest that instead of claiming the whole amount of the goods, you accept a sum of US$ 150 as the salvage value of the goods should be at least US$ 50. In case you agree to it please let us know and we shall immediately arrange our remittance.

Thanking you.

Yours faithfully,
Sd/-
Manager

Asking Insurance Broker to Effect a Floating Policy

INTERNATIONAL TRADERS
Panjim

13th Sept., 19___

Messrs Tardeo & Sons,
Panjim.

Dear Sirs,

This has reference to the personal visit of your representative to our office on 11th September, 19 __. We have decided to accept your quotation of 1%. Please, therefore, cover us for US$ accept your quotation of 1%. Please, therefore, cover us for US$ 1% on all goods in transit to or from our showroom to any part of India. This should include goods in train and on railway stations, goods in transport and in godowns of transport offices and goods in postal transit.

A cheque for US $50 being the amount of premium is enclosed.

Thank you.

Yours faithfully,
For International Traders,
Sd/-
Manager

Encl: Cheque

Insurance Company's Letter to its Agents Advising to Stop Further Insurance

CENTRAL INSURANCE COMPANY
Indonesia

16th May, 19___

M/s. Rajneesh Insurance Agency,
Indonesia.

Dear Sirs,

We appreciate your efforts in procuring substantial business for us during the last few years against risk of fire and pilferage. However, in view of recent troubles arising in the State regarding bifurcation, we are not in a position to undertake any more risks. We, therefore, advise you to please refrain from accepting any further liability on our behalf in the whole of Andhra Pradesh State until further advice.

Thank you.

Yours faithfully,
Sd/-
Central Insurance Company,
Indonesia

D. CAR/SCOOTER INSURANCE

Correspondence regarding this subject is death with under the chapter "Correspondence Regarding Motor Vehicles".

22

Correspondence Regarding Motor Vehicles

Application for the Purchase of a Car/Scooter

To,

M/s. PLS Motors,
Hong Kong.

Dear Sirs,

Please book my/our order for a Scooter/Car and let me/ us know the allocation number of the order. I/We forward here with a Post Office Savings Bank Pass Book to show that I/We have opened a Security Deposit Account in (name of post office)........... Post Office for US $50 for a Scooter and US $4.00 for a Car (this is however subject to change from time to time) pledged in your favour which will not be withdrawn by me/us except on a written authority from you at the time when the vehicle is ready for delivery.

The Order requisites are given below:—

1. Full name of the Applicant ______________________________

2. Address of the Applicant______________________________

3. Father's/Husband's name ______________________________

4. Vocation______________________________

5. Whether the Applicant pays income-tax____________________

6. Whether the Applicant owns or has owned any scooter/car, is so the date of purchase and sale if any of the last scooter/car______________

7. Whether the Applicant has registered for a Scooter/Car with any other dealer (if the answer is 'yes' the particulars of the order should be

stated) ____

____

8. No and date of the Post Office Security Deposit Account ______

____

I/We do solemnly affirm and declare that I/We have not purchased a new scooter/car during this calendar year.

Yours faithfully,

....

Allocation No. (Signature of the applicant)

Note : Application form must be fowarded with a Post Office Savings Bank Pass Book to show that a Security Deposit Account for US $50 or 400 has been opened in a Post Office and pledged in favour of M/s. PLS Motors, Hong Kong; otherwise order will not be registered. Booking restricted to residents of Hong Kong only.

Reply to the Above

FOR OFFICE USE ONLY

Date...............

PLS MOTORS,
Hong Kong.

Dear Sir,

We acknowledge receipt of your order for a scooter car against allocation number...........which please quote in all future correspondence.

Thank you.

Yours faithfully,
For PLS Motors, Hong Kong
Sd/-
Manager

Name & Address of Applicant

____

____

____

Sale Letter for a Car/Scooter

Dated................

To

The Motor Licensing Officer.

Dear Sir,

_____ This is to certify that I/we have sold my/our Car/Motor Cycle/ Scooter ____

to ____

of (Address) _______________________________________

on date)_______________________ Kindly transfer ownership of the above to ____________________

Thank you.

Yours faithfully,
Sd/-

Receipt of Money for Sale of a Car Scooter

Dated............

Re: Sale of ____

Regd. No ____________________________________.

Received with thanks from ____________________________ the sum of US$ _________(US$______________________by cash/cheque No. ________________dated __________________on_________________in full and final payment/toward advance of my ____________Car/Scooter Registered No. ___________The Car/Scooter is my/our absolute property free from all encumbrances and taxes are paid up-to-date. The Car/Scooter is sold and delivered in perfect running order and condition, as seen, tried and approved, and as it stands today.

20 Cent Revenue Stamp.
Signature & Address.

____

____

Delivery Receipt of Car/Scooter

I have this ________day of ________________taken the delivery of one ____________scooter/car registered bearing Engine No.

________________Chasis No. ___________second hand registered No.___________from Mr.______________in perfect order and condition as approved after test, the necessary documents relating to the sale of the scooter/car as well as the tools and equipment as per settlement. And in full and final payment of the above mentioned car/scooter, I/we have paid/ agreed to pay the sum of US$____________to_______.

I shall be responsible to pay all further taxes for which you will not be liable here-in-after this date.

Delivery time_______Remarks______________Payment of Rs.__________________has been as follows by cash/cheque No. ______________on_________________

Place____________ Signature_______________

Date_______________ Address______________________

Intimation of Transfer of Ownership of Motor Vehicle

FORM

(Rules...........under the Motor Vehicles Rules 19____)

Intimation of Transfer of ownership of a Motor Vehicle.

1. (1) I,_____________________________son of _______________of (2) ___________-forward herewith the certificate of registration and the certificate of fitness (3) of Motor Vehicle No.____(4) the ownership of which has been transferred to me by (5)___________________-and hereby request that the said vehicle may be registered in my name and that the certificate of registration and the certificate of fitness (6) be amended accordingly.

Date of purchase__________________19 _________________________
(Dated)

(Signature or thumb impression of the transferee.)

Endorsement in the case of vehicle which is the subject of an agreement of Hire-Purchase

I/we (1) being a party to an agreement of Hire-purchase in respect of vehicle specified above, consent to the transfer of ownership of the said vehicle to (2)__________________with whom I/we (3) have entered into an agreement of hire-purchase in respect of this vehicle.

(Signature of the party other than the Owner.)

(Date)

Letter to the Superintendent of Police asking for getting a Duplicate R.C. Book

To,

The Superintendent of Police,
Bangkok.

Re : R.C. Book for my Car No. B.L.V. 1237

Dear Sir,

The R.C. book of my Car No. B.L.V. 1237 has been lost and the Affidavit sworn by me is enclosed.

I shall be glad if you would kindly arrange to get me the new R.C. Book

Thank you.

Yours faithfully,
Sd/-
General Manager
Super Mills

Encl: as Above.

Letter from the Superintendent of Police to the Registering Authority for the Issue of a Duplicate R.C. Book.

Office of the Superintendent of Police, M.V. Section, Bangkok.

Memo No. 1214/MVS, Bangkok. 23rd August, 19_

To,

The Registering Authority,
M.V. Dept., Bangkok.

Sub: Issue of Duplicate R.C. Book of vehicle No. BLV 1237.

Mr. R.D. Jones, owner of the above-noted car, has applied for issue of duplicate R.C. Book. Petition for issue of the Duplicate R.C. book is enclosed herewith. Kindly issue the same.

Sd/-
Registering Authority,
Bangkok

Copy to:

R.D. Jones,
Super Mills,
Bangkok.

Affidavit for Above Letter

IN THE COURT OF MAGISTRATE, FIRST CLASS
Bangkok

Stamp for Rs. 3.20

AFFIDAVIT

I, R.D. Jones, son of Shri S.R. Jones, aged about 38 years, by faith Christian, by profession Service, at present General Manager, Super Mills, Bangkok, do hereby solemnly declare and affirm as follows:—

(1) That the Owner Book of Car No. BLV 1237 stands in the name of my wife, Mrs. Tony Jones.

(2) That the above-mentioned Owner Book was seized by the A.S.I. A. Willam, on 25-1-19 ___ in connection with Tong P.S. Case No. 12 (1) 74 u/s. 279/304-A.I.P.S. pending in the Court of Mr. M.N. George, M.M. 1st Class, Bangkok.

(3) That the said Owner Book is not traceable in the above Court.

(4) That search was made for the above Owner Book at the Bangkok also but it could not be traced.

VERIFICATION

I do hereby solemnly declare that the Statements made above are true to the best of my knowledge, information and belief. I signed this at Bangkok on 11-7-19——

Sd/-
R.D. Jones
11-7-19____

The deponent, R.D. Jones,
solemnly affirmed before me who is identified by Mr. K
Collins, Advocate Bangkok.

Sd/-
Magistrate.
1st Class, Bangkok.

Complaint Regarding a Defect in Repair of a Car

M. Chand
Galib Street
Karachi, Pakistan.

(Date)

Yusuf Motors,
Karachi.

Dear Sirs,

I regret very much to say that the steering wheel of my car No. DHB 1637 is still as stiff as it was before it was given to you for repairing. I am sending the same through my driver and shall appreciate your repairing it immediately.

Thank you.

Yours faithfully,
Sd/-
M. Chand

Reply to the above

Yusuf MOTORS
Karachi

Mr. M. Chand,
14, Galib Street,
Karachi, Pakistan.

Dear Sir,

We thank you for your letter dated......

We sincerely regret that through an oversight the steering wheel of your car remained untouched at the time of repairs. However, the needful has now been done.

We assure you once again of our best services always.

Thank of.

Yours faithfully,
For Yusuf Motors,
Sd/-
Manager

---

23 Import & Export Correspondence

Letter of an Inquiry

BRITISH TEA & COFFEE CENTRE.
London

23rd May, 19——

Messrs Emkay Tea Co.
London.

Dear Sirs,

We understand that you are one of the largest exporters of tea in India. Every month we import as much as 50,000 lbs. of tea and 20,000 lbs. of coffee from the Indian merchants of Calcutta. We are always short of requirements and may times we have to import these articles from other Asian countries, like Indonesia, Ceylon, etc. We shall be glad to know if you are in a position to supply us at least 15,000 lbs. of tea every month. In case you can supply us this much quantity, please send us your trade terms and samples for our examination.

Yours faithfully,
Sd/-
For British Tea & Coffee Centre.

Reply to the Above

EMKAY TEA COMPANY
London

10th June, 19___

Messrs British Tea and Coffee Centre,
Tea & Coffee Merchants,
London.

Dear Sirs,

We thank you for your letter dated 23rd May, 19—,

We have pleasure in informing you that we can supply you any quantity up to 22,500 lbs. every month.

Owing to present fluctuations in the tea market, the prices are generally changing every now and then. However, we shall be willing to enter into an agreement for a period of three months after which the agreement will be renewed keeping in view the latest market trend.

Present market price, *i.e.* the price at which we shall be willing to enter into an initial agreement for three months is £1.50 per lb.

We have today despatched by Air Mail three packets of the samples. Although the varieties are different, the price is the same, i.e. £ 1.50 per lb

We hope you will find the above varieties of tea suitable and shall write to us at your earliest on receipt of which, we shall send you our Draft Agreement for our final approval.

Yours faithfully,
Sd/-
For Emkay Tea Cos.,

Asking for a Catalogue and Trade Terms

KEATS BROTHERS
43, Church Gate
London (UK).

2nd May, 19—

Messrs A. Whiteman & Co,
Plastic Sheets Manufacturers,
New York (U.S.A.).

Dear Sirs,

As you may be aware, we are one of the biggest importers of Plastic Sheets in UK. Our annual imports exceed £ million and our regular suppliers are: Benrai & Co., London, M/s. Greaves Bros., London, M/s. William & Co., New York, and M/s. Eklund & Co Ltd. New York. Of late our consumption has increased owing to installation of one more machine at our factory and hence the necessity of contacting other suppliers for import.

We have been dealing with all these parties for the last twenty years and they shall be gland to give you any reference or reply to any inquiry you may ask for.

May we please request you to send us your catalogue along with your very best terms?

Yours faithfully,
For Keats Brothers,
Sd/-

Reply to the Above

A. WHITEMAN & CO.
Plastic Sheets Manufacturers,
New York (U.S.A.)

23rd May, 19____

Messrs Keats Brothers,
43, Church Gate,
London (UK).

Dear Sirs,

We thank you for your letter dated 2nd May, 19——.

We have today sent under separate post a complete catalogue along with our trade terms.

Needless to say, you will find our prices very competitive and quality much better than many other exporters on account of our being pioneers in the trade of manufacturing plastic sheets.

A packet of samples will be sent within two or three days.

We shall now await your valued order which will take our most careful and prompt attention for its execution.

Yours faithfully,
For A. Whiteman & Co.,
Sd/-

Letter Ordering Goods

KEATS BROTHERS
43, Church Gate,
London (UK).

2nd June, 19____

Messrs A Whiteman & Co.,
Plastic Sheet Manufacturers,
New York (U.S.A.).

Dear Sirs,

We thank you for your letterhead 23rd May, 19—-

We have also received your catalogue and samples sent by you separately.

We have pleasure in placing with you an order for the following goods :-

1.	Rose Red Sheets	'No. XXI-A'	1000 lbs.
2.	Dark Red Sheets	'No. LLI-F'	2000 lbs.
3.	Sky Blue Sheets	'No. SBI-C'	1000 lbs.
4.	Yellow Sheets	'No. YL-C'	15000 lbs.
5.	Light Green Sheets	'No. LGI-C'	2000 lbs.
6.	Dark Green Sheets.	No DGI-C'	2000 lbs.

Goods should be sent in wooden cases.

Delivery is required by the middle of August, 19—

Thank you.

Yours faithfully,
For Sushil Brothers,
Sd/-

Acknowledge an Order

A. WHITEMAN & CO.
Plastic Sheets Manufacturers
New York, (U.S.A.)

15th June, 19—-

Messrs Keats Brothers,
43, Church Gate,
London (UK).

Dear Sirs,

We thank you for your valued order dated 2nd June, 19—.

The goods are being packed and shall be sent by S.S. 'INDIANACA' leaving New York on 25th June, 19—, reaching Bombay during the first week of August—.

Necessary shipping documents will be sent in due course.

Thanking you and assuring you of our best co-operation.

Yours faithfully,
For A. Whiteman & co.
sd/-

Letter Intimating the Execution of an Order

A WHITEMAN & CO.
Plastic Sheets Manufacturers
New York (U.S.A.)

30th June, 19—-

Messrs Keats Brothers,
43, Church Gate,
London (UK).

Dear Sirs,

With further reference to our letter dated the 15th June, 19— we have pleasure on informing you that the goods have been shipped on your account by S.S. 'INDIANACA', and necessary invoice for £3000 is enclosed. We trust the goods will meet your approval.

We have drawn on you '90' days' at sight through the City Bank of New York against this shipment and we hope you will clear the draft in time.

Thanking you and assuring you of our best co-operation.

Yours faithfully,
For A. Whiteman & Co.,
Sd/-

Prior Intimation about the arrival of Shipment by the Branch of Booking Agency

GRAY & SONS.
12, P.M. Road,
New York.

2nd August, 19—

Messrs Keats Brothers,
40, Church Gate,
London (UK).

Dear Sirs,

We are informed by our head office that the steamship 'INDIANACA' by which cases of your plastic sheets have been shipped is due in New York harbour on the 7th August, 19—. The exact time of arrival will be notified in all English Dailies of the 6th August, 19-. We request you to please await the arrival and arrange to take the delivery immediately on the arrival of the ship.

Yours faithfully,
M. Williams.
Manager

Letter for a Bank Regarding Payment of Draft

CITY BANK OF NEW YORK
P.M. Road, New York

6th August, 19—

Messrs Keats Brothers,
43, Church Gate,
London (UK)

Sub: Our L C / No. 112 for £3000 due on 2nd November 19— relating to 25 cases of merchandise per S.S. 'INDIANACA', arriving tomorrow.

Dear Sirs,

With reference to the above Draft, we have to request you to please let us know by return of post whether you want us to clear and store the relative goods.

In case the goods are to be cleared and stored in a Duty-Paid Warehouse, a sum of £550 must be remitted to us along with your reply.

If we do not hear from you within four days, we shall have the goods cleared and stored in Bond.

Yours faithfully,
H.O. Scott
(Agent)

Informing a Client Regarding Allotment of Stalls in the Exhibition

ALL INDONESIA EXHIBITION FOR SMALL INDUSTRIES
Exhibition Ground
Jakarta.

Dated: March, 4, 19__

Express Delivery (Post)

To,

M/s Surya Bros.
Jahan Karya,
Jakarta.

Re: Allotment of small stalls of 10' x 10'.

Dear Sirs,

It has been decided by the Executive committee of the all Indonesia. Exhibition of Small Industries to allot the shopping stalls to the applicants by draw of lots on industry wise basis. For example, if there are 25 applicants from one industry, say soap manufacturing, the draw will be made from these applicants and the shops allotted accordingly.

The draw will be held on the 19th March, 19—, at 2.30 P.M. in the Administrative Block of the Exhibition. The decision taken on this date will be final and binding on all parties.

Your are requested to kindly make it convenient to be present or depute your representative to witness the draw of lots.

Thank you.

Yours faithfully,
Sd/-
Exhibition Officer.

Extermination of White Ants

Phone: 568827

PEST CONTROL SERVICES OF USA
(Insect Control & Pesticides)
2655, Bank Street, New York,
USA

PSI/WA 1078-70

Dated: 7th August, 19—

Scott Pocket Books,
31/1, Free Street,
New York.

Re: Extermination of white ants.

Dear Sirs,

We thank you for your letter dated 4th August, 19—

Since, our representatives have inspected the premises, and we have pleasure to enclose herewith our usual service contract for the proposed treatment. Kindly sign the duplicate copy of the service contract form and return the same to us to enable us to carry out the necessary treatment to prevent your valuable property.

Thanking you and assuring you of our best and prompt services at all times. We remain,

Yours faithfully,
For Pest Control Services of USA,
Prop.

Contract for Extermination of White Ants

Phone: 568827

PEST CONTROL SERVICES OF USA
(Insect Control & Pesticides),
2655 Bank Street, New York,
USA

Service Contract No. 102/570
Between Pest Control Services of USA, and
Scott Pocket Books,
31/1, Free Street,
New York.

1. In consideration of the sum of US $100 (Dollar One hundred only) to be paid by M/s. Komal Pocket Books (hereinafter called "OWNERS") to M/s. Pest Control Services of India or their representative or agents (herinafter called "CONTRACTORS"), the contractors shall treat the premises mentioned in Schedule I to the extent necessary to free the said premises of the presence of white ants.

2. If at any item or times after the completion of the initial treatment white ants reappear in the said premises the owners shall promptly inform the contractors and the contractors shall repeat the treatment or take other measures without any further payment before the month of August 9— to free the said premises of the presence of white ants.

3. The contractors shall not by any means be or become liable to the owners directly for any damages whatsoever.

4. The owner shall pay to the contractors the full amount of the charges mentioned in paragraph I hereinafter at the signing this contract.

5. Monthly inspections will be carried out by the contractors and treatment will be given, if found necessary.

SCHEDULE I

Your two godowns and the entire office premises situated at the above state address.

Date.....

For and on behalf of owners for
Pest Controls Services of USA,
Prop.

Certificate of Insurance

MOTOR VEHICLES ACT, 1930 (USA)

I.Y.I

Certificate of Insurance

Certificate No. D 7394/CMB. 000668A/67

1. Registration Mark and Number or NYI 8449
   Description of the vehicle Insured
2. Name and address of Insured
   Mr. G. George
   31/2, Church Street,
   New York.
3. Effective date of Commencement of Insurance for the purpose of the Act 15-2-19
4. Date of expiry of Insurance 14-2-19
5. Person or classes of persons entitled to drive.

   Any person.

The insured may also drive a Motor Cycle not belonging to him and not hired to him under a Hire-Purchase Agreement.

Provided the person driving holds a licence to drive the vehicle or has held and is not disqualified for holding or obtaining such a licence.

6. Limitation as to use:

   The Policy covers use for any propose other than

   (a) Hire or reward

   (b) Organised racing or speed testing.

I/WE hereby certify that the policy to which the certificate relates as well as this Certificate of Insurance are issued in accordance with the provisions of Chapter VIII of the Motor Vehicles Act, 1930.

(Authorised Insurer)

Examined.........

Lost Certificate

An Affidavit for a lost Certificate of Insurance is necessary only is those cases, where a policy is terminated before its normal expiry date and the current Certificate of Insurance cannot be found.

If a Certificate of Insurance is lost during the currency of a policy, and a duplicate may be issued under the provisions of the Motor Vehicles Act, 1930, provided the Insured lodges a Declaration stating full particulars of the circumstances connected with the loss or destruction and agrees to return the original certificate if found and pays a fee of US $1.00.

NOTES

NOTES

NOTES